CHARLES SPURGEON

DISCOVERING
THE POWER OF
CHRIST
THE
WARRIOR

CHARLES SPURGEON

DISCOVERING
THE POWER OF
CHRIST
THE
WARRIOR

COMPILED AND EDITED BY
LANCE WUBBELS

P.O. BOX 635, LYNNWOOD, WA 98046

Scripture quotations are taken from the King James Version of the Bible.

About the Author

CHARLES HADDON SPURGEON (1834–1892) was the remarkable British "Boy Preacher of the Fens" who became one of the truly greatest preachers of all time. Coming from a flourishing country pastorate in 1854, he accepted a call to pastor London's New Park Street Chapel. This building soon proved too small and so work on Spurgeon's Metropolitan Tabernacle was begun in 1859. Meanwhile his weekly sermons were being printed and having a remarkable sale—25,000 copies every week in 1865 and translated into more than twenty languages.

Spurgeon built the Metropolitan Tabernacle into a congregation of over 6,000 and added well over 14,000 members during his thirty-eight-year London ministry. The combination of his clear voice, his mastery of language, his sure grasp of Scripture, and a deep love for Christ produced some of the noblest preaching of any age. An astounding 3,561 sermons have been preserved in sixty-three volumes, *The New Park Street Pulpit* and *The Metropolitan Tabernacle Pulpit,* from which the chapters of this book have been selected and edited.

During his lifetime, Spurgeon is estimated to have preached to 10,000,000 people. He remains history's most widely read preacher. There is more available material written by Spurgeon than by any other Christian author, living or dead. His sixty-three volumes of sermons stand as the largest set of books by a single author in the history of Christianity, comprising the equivalent to the twenty-seven volumes of the ninth edition of the *Encyclopedia Britannica.*

About the Editor

LANCE WUBBELS is the managing editor of Bethany House Publishers. His interest in the writings of Charles Spurgeon began while doing research on an editorial project that required extensive reading of Spurgeon's sermons. He discovered a wealth of sermon classics that are filled with practical, biblical insight for every believer and written in a timeless manner that makes them as relevant today as the day they were spoken. His desire is to select and present Spurgeon's writings in a way that will appeal to a wide audience of readers and allow one of the greatest preachers of all time to enrich believers' lives.

Wubbels is the author of *The Gentle Hills* fiction series with Bethany House Publishers, a four-book series that is set during World War II, as well as the heartwarming short novel, *One Small Miracle*. A naturally gifted storyteller, he captures readers with a warm, homey style filled with wit and insight that appeals to a wide readership.

Contents

Introduction

THE EULOGIES OF CHARLES Spurgeon's preaching are almost endless. It is a preaching legacy that can never be forgotten; it may never be surpassed. Considered by his peers then and now as "The Prince of Preachers," Spurgeon will stand for many years to come as the epitome of pulpit mastery. Joseph Parker, another of London's famous preachers, wrote: "Mr. Spurgeon's career has proved that evangelical teaching can draw around itself the greatest congregation in the world, and hold it for a lifetime.... The great voice has ceased. It was the mightiest voice I ever heard."

It was said that the sermons of Charles Spurgeon were born in an atmosphere charged with the Holy Spirit. Spurgeon said "more than once we were all so awestruck with the solemnity of the meeting, that we sat silent for some moments, while the Lord's power appeared to overshadow us." Perhaps that explains why the British Prime Minister W. E. Gladstone, members of the royal family, and members of Parliament would attend his church when it had become known as a "church of shopkeepers." Undoubtedly, the combination of a beautiful speaking voice, a dramatic flair and style that was captivating, a profound depth and breadth of spirituality, as well as a powerful commitment to a biblical theology go a long way to explaining how he took the city of London by storm. But this passionate biblical expositor was always quick to credit his success to the powerful work of the Holy Spirit.

Billy Graham has described Charles Spurgeon as "a preacher who extolled Jesus Christ—everlastingly!" And it is my firm belief that few biblical themes inspired Spurgeon to extol Christ more than the fact that Jesus is the Almighty Warrior who went forth to war against evil and has wrought a marvelous victory over every evil foe that we can ever meet. Through His death and resurrection, Christ has met the prince of darkness and all the powers of evil that set themselves against Him, and we know how He fought with them, overcame them, and trampled them beneath His feet. And even now, as the Head of the Church, Christ is still warring against sin, struggling most strenuously to drive sin out of the world, and to make the earth His own dominion wherein He shall reign in righteousness and peace.

Listen as Spurgeon vividly describes two of the cruelest and greatest enemies that we will ever face—death and hell: "Death is a land of darkness, as darkness itself, without any order, yet a sovereign eye surveys it, and a master hand holds its key. Hell also is a horrible region, where powers of evil and of terror hold their high court and dread assembly; but hell trembles at the presence of the Lord, and there is a throne higher than the throne of evil. Let us rejoice that nothing in heaven, or earth, or in places under the earth is left to itself to create anarchy. Everywhere, serene above the floods, the Lord sits as King forever and ever. No province of the universe is free from the divine rule. Things do not come by chance. Nowhere does chance and chaos reign, nowhere is evil really and permanently enthroned. Rest assured that the Lord has prepared His throne in the heavens, and His kingdom rules over all; for if the lower hell and death are subject to His government, much more all things that are on this lower world."

The fact that Jesus Christ is now reigning in heaven brought great excitement to the preaching of Charles Spurgeon. He paints a marvelous picture of how all the angels and principalities and powers in the heavenly places pay their loyal homage to Jesus as their Lord forever, but Spurgeon does not stop there. He declares the extension of the reign of Christ as over all things. Absolute providence and rule are seen in the hands of Christ the King as He takes the keys of death and hell and rightfully rules and manages over all the matters of the grave and overrules all the councils of hell, restraining the mischievous devices of Satan or turning them to subserve His own designs of good. Christ's kingdom extends over all existences in whatever regions they may be.

Come along with Spurgeon as he continues to extol Jesus Christ as the One seen as the unconquerable King in the book of Daniel, as the mighty Savior of Isaiah's vision, and as the magnificent Lamb of glory described by John in his book of Revelation.

Not only does Spurgeon declare Christ as the destroyer of death but as the destroyer of Satan. Christ is seen as the great liberator of His people, freeing them from their sins and their bondages to sin. He is pictured as the omnipotent leader of His Church today in reaching the world and as the One who will ride forth on the white horse to bring final judgment upon all of creation through His second coming.

I invite you to read these twelve select chapters as you would listen to a trusted and skilled pastor. The implications of the rock-solid truth of Spurgeon's teaching are so staggering that I pray the Holy Spirit will open your eyes to it. We never need fear death, or the devil, or the future, or the present. Spurgeon will meet you where you live, and you will not be disappointed.

Careful editing has helped to sharpen the focus of these sermons while retaining the authentic and timeless flavor they undoubtedly bring.

The psalmist's petition is "Gird thy sword upon thy thigh, O most mighty." When a soldier intends to use his sword, he puts it where he can easily get at it; he hangs it by his side so that he can readily draw it from its scabbard when he needs it either for attack or for defense. So the prayer means, "Lord, use Your Word; put power and energy into the truth as it is proclaimed." The preaching of a sermon may be like the drawing of a sword from its scabbard. Just as the soldier's sword kills nobody until the soldier grasps its hilt with a firm grip and deals the deadly blow with it, so will the sermon not be really effective until Christ puts His hand to the Word. Here is the sword of the Spirit, like some ancient weapon hanging on the wall of an old castle; but O thou blessed King of kings, will You not take it in Your almighty hand and prove again what You can do with it? Right and left You will cut and thrust with it and so receive a glorious victory over all the powers of evil. If Christ shall send His Word home to your heart, you will soon perceive that it is a very different thing from what it is when we poor mortals only preach it in your ears. When we blow the gospel trumpet at Ear-gate, you perhaps take no notice; but if the Prince Emmanuel shall bring the great battering ram of His cross up to Heart-cast and smite it blow after blow, the posts will rock, the bars will snap, the gate will fall, and the Prince will ride in and reign forever over the soul that He has won by His grace as long ago He bought it with His blood. Oh, that He would do it at this very moment!

Chapter One

The Almighty Warrior

Gird thy sword upon thy thigh, O most mighty, with thy glory and thy majesty. And in thy majesty ride prosperously because of truth and meekness and righteousness; and thy right hand shall teach thee terrible things. Thine arrows are sharp in the heart of the king's enemies; whereby the people fall under thee
—Psalm 45:3–5.

PSALM 45 HAS BEEN THOUGHT by some to be a marriage song for Solomon on the occasion of his wedding with the daughter of Pharaoh. It may be so, but more importantly we find in the psalm a distinct reference to the Lord Jesus Christ and to His marriage union with His Church. Under the Mosaic dispensation, when a man had married a wife, he was not to go out to war for a year, but when the Lord Jesus Christ entered into a marriage union with His people, that very union made it necessary that He should wage war on their behalf. He had to meet all their spiritual foes in terrible conflict. The prince of darkness and all the powers of evil set themselves in array against Him, and we know how He fought with them, overcame them, and trampled them beneath His feet as the treader of grapes crushes the purple clusters in the winepress. And now, even though in heaven He is in a state of rest, yet here, as the Head of the Church, His mystical body, He is still warring against sin, struggling most strenuously to drive sin out of the world and to make the earth His own dominion wherein He shall reign in righteousness and peace.

The prayer of the psalmist, as we have it in our text, is a suitable petition for us also to present. We desire to stir up our almighty Champion to go forth to war against evil. How gloriously He went forth with His first disciples in the brave days of old! They rode forth to battle and to death under His leadership, but it was to victory too in those glorious times of conflict and conquest. But we seem to have fallen upon days of peace, that false peace that arises from lethargy, stagnation, and death. We have need to cry mightily to the great Captain of our salvation to gird His sword upon His thigh, to order His great war chariot to be brought to the front again, that He may ride forth to battle again with all His attendant hosts, that His enemies may know that His power is as great as ever it was in the ages that are gone.

The Warrior Armed

"Gird thy sword upon thy thigh, O most mighty, with thy glory and thy majesty." So *Christ has a sword.* What is it? Certainly not the sword of which soldiers and princes are so proud, for it was concerning that kind that Jesus said to Peter, "Put up again thy sword into his place: for all they that take the sword shall perish with the sword" (Matt. 26:52). It was concerning that sort of weapon that Jesus said to Pilate, "My kingdom is not of this world: if my kingdom were of this world, then would my servants fight" (John 18:36). Christ could truly say that the weapons of His warfare were not carnal but were mighty through God to the pulling down of strongholds. His was not the fighting that needs sword and spear and shield and buckler as the world's warriors use. His wrestling was "not against flesh and blood, but against principalities, against powers, against the rulers of the darkness of this world, against spiritual wickedness in high places" (Eph. 6:12). The main weapon that Christ wielded was "the sword of the Spirit, which is the word of God" (Eph. 6:17).

The psalmist prayed, "Gird thy sword upon thy thigh." But in the book of Revelation we read concerning Christ, "out of his mouth went a sharp two-edged sword" (Rev. 1:16). You know how constantly Jesus quoted the Scriptures in resisting Satan's temptation or the assaults of His human adversaries. "It is written" was His unanswerable argument at all times (Matt. 4). This sword, which Christ wields, is not made of steel to cut human bodies; it is a sword of truth to pierce the hearts and consciences of sinners. It is said to be sharp, "sharper than any two-edged sword, piercing even to the dividing asunder of soul and spirit, and of the joints and marrow, and is a discerner of the thoughts and intents of the heart" (Heb. 4:12).

No other sword wounds as the sword of the Spirit does; it wounds so that none but God can heal. You may bring it down upon a heart that is harder than a millstone, but its edge will never be turned, and it will cut the stone in two. It is a sharp, wounding sword, and it is a killing sword. Wherever it goes, it kills sin, cuts iniquity in pieces, slays self-righteousness, and destroys the weaknesses of the flesh. This sword is also two-edged. A sword with only one edge to it has a blunt back, but the sword of the Spirit has no blunt backstroke. In fact, it cuts always, and every part of it is keen as a razor's edge. Promises, precepts, doctrines, threatenings are all sharp and penetrating; there is no part of the Word of God that is ineffective to produce the result for which it was given.

Notice that the psalmist prays, "Gird *thy sword* upon thy thigh." The Bible is not your Bible or mine alone, it is God's Bible, it is Christ's Bible, it is the Holy Spirit's Bible. Truth is no monopoly; it is not the priest's truth, it is the people's truth, it is everyone's truth, but it is most of all Christ's truth. Why is it that the Word of God is Christ's sword? Surely it is because that Word tells us about Him; He is the text of which the Bible is the sermon. The Bible is like a signpost pointing to Him and saying, "This is the way to Jesus Christ."

Holy Scripture gives you a wardrobe full of choice garments, and they all smell of myrrh and aloe and cassia because Christ has worn them. The Word of God is specially Christ's because He has used it and still uses it. My use of the Word will have very little effect unless Christ uses me as the instrument by which He shows what He can do with it. Someone looked at the sword of a famous conqueror and, after examining it closely, said, "I do not see anything special about it." "No," was the answer, "perhaps not. But if you could see the brawny arm that wielded it, you would understand why it is so notable." So is it with the sword of the Spirit, this divinely inspired Book. It may not seem to you as though it could work such wonders as it is continually doing, but if you could see the hand of Christ that wields that sword, you would understand where the glory and the majesty of the truth are found and where it derives its power to convince and convert the sons of men.

The psalmist's petition is *"Gird thy sword upon thy thigh, O most mighty."* When a soldier intends to use his sword, he puts it where he can easily get at it; he hangs it by his side so that he can readily draw it from its scabbard when he needs it either for attack or for defense. So the prayer means, "Lord, use Your Word; put power and energy into the truth as it is proclaimed." The preaching of a sermon may be like the drawing of a sword from its scabbard. Just as the soldier's sword kills nobody until the soldier grasps its hilt with a firm grip and deals the deadly blow with it, so will the sermon not be really effective until Christ puts His hand to the Word. Here is the sword of the Spirit, like some ancient weapon hanging on the wall of an old castle; but O thou blessed King of kings, will You not take it in Your almighty hand and prove again what You can do with it? Right and left You will cut and thrust with it and so receive a glorious victory over all the powers of evil. If Christ shall send His Word home to your heart, you will soon perceive that it is a very different thing from what it is when we poor mortals only preach it in your ears. When we blow the gospel trumpet at Ear-gate, you perhaps take no notice; but if the Prince Emmanuel shall bring the great battering ram of His cross up to Heart-cast and smite it blow after blow, the posts will rock, the bars will snap, the gate will fall, and the Prince will ride in and reign forever over the soul that He has won by His grace as long ago He bought it with His blood. Oh, that He would do it at this very moment!

Notice the title that the psalmist gives to the almighty Warrior: *"O most mighty."* Christ not only is mighty but is also most mighty. There have been mighty men in prayer, but He is the most mighty Advocate with His Father on His people's behalf. There have been mighty preachers of the Word, but "never man spake like this man" (John 7:46). There have been many friends of sinners, but there has never been such a friend of sinners as Jesus is. Your sins are mighty to destroy, but He is more mighty to save. I will grant you that your passions are mighty, that is positive; I will grant you that they are more mighty than you are, that is comparative; but Jesus is most mighty to overcome them, and that is superlative. The superlative might of the love of Christ as shown in His death upon the cross is infinitely greater than the positive and comparative might of our actual sin and the depravity of our nature. May He prove Himself most mighty in winning us to Himself!

The psalmist not only prays to the Lord to gird His sword upon His thigh but also adds, *"with thy glory and thy majesty."* Did you ever see Christ in His glory and His majesty? I know that you have never seen Him this way unless you have first seen yourself in your degradation and shame. There, where the poor, broken-hearted sinner lies prostrate in the dust, feeling himself to be less than nothing, the great Conqueror comes in His glory and majesty and says to him, "I am your salvation. I have loved you with an everlasting love and laid down my life that I might save you."

Perhaps you remember how John Bunyan pictures Prince Emmanuel's entry in Mansoul after he had captured it from Diabolus: "This was the manner of going up thither. He was clad in his golden armor, he rode in his royal chariot, the trumpets sounded about him, the colors were displayed, his ten thousands went up at his feet, and the elders of Mansoul danced before him." They might well rejoice at His coming in glory and majesty to take up His dwelling in their midst and to prove to them how fully He had forgiven their rebellion now that they had repented of their sin and accepted Him as their right Lord and Savior. So will it be with all who welcome Christ into their hearts and no longer yield allegiance to the prince of darkness.

The Chariot Filled

"And in thy majesty ride prosperously because of truth and meekness and righteousness." The Eastern monarch stood erect in his war chariot and rode forth in great splendor in the midst of his troops. To my mind, the preaching of the gospel is the chariot of our Lord Jesus Christ. The gospel itself is His sword; and the preaching of the gospel, the distribution of the Word, by which Christ is made known to the sons of men, may be likened to His chariot of salvation. This chariot appears to have four wheels; or, if you like, you can call them the four pure white steeds that draw the gospel chariot; their names, according to the text, are majesty, truth, meekness, and righteousness. These are the four supports of the gospel, or the four motive powers by which the gospel of Christ is brought into the hearts of sinners.

The power of the gospel lies first in *the majesty of Christ*. Jesus Christ, the Son of Mary, is also the Son of God, who could truly say, "I and my Father are one" (John 10:30). He who died on Calvary's cross is the King of kings and Lord of lords. That very man who cried in agony, "I thirst" (John 19:28), is the almighty God who holds the waters in the hollow of His hand. Does this not move us to trust Him? The majesty of Christ should win not only your admiration but also your affection. He whose face was more marred than that of any other man was the One of whom Isaiah said, "His name shall be called Wonderful, Counsellor, The mighty God, The everlasting Father, The Prince of Peace" (Isa. 9:6). Does not this fact melt your heart to Christ, that He, against whom you have sinned, should have suffered for your sins and borne the curse and penalty that were due to you? Surely the majesty of Christ should lead you to trust Him.

The next wheel of the chariot is *truth*. The gospel is absolute truth. Whatever there is in the world that is false, this certainly is a positive fact: "Christ Jesus came into the world to save sinners" (1 Tim. 1:15). It is also true that He will receive you if you come to Him; come and trust Him and see whether He will not welcome you. It is true that He can forgive the blackest offenses and that He does forgive all who sincerely repent of their sin and trust in His atoning sacrifice. It is true that He can uproot sin from the heart, make the unholy holy, and cause the disobedient to become obedient to God's commands. This is not a matter of conjecture on our part; it is no guesswork, no dream of an excited imagination. Many of us have proved the sanctifying power of the doctrines of the cross, and we therefore urge you to prove this for yourself, that the truth of the gospel may commend itself to you.

The next wheel of the chariot is *meekness*. Jesus said, "Learn of me; for I am meek and lowly in heart" (Matt. 11:29). It is no proud Savior who invites you to come to Him. Let me remind you working-men that Jesus Christ belonged to your rank in life and probably toiled at the carpenter's bench with Joseph, the husband of His mother. Jesus was no domineering aristocrat, looking down with contempt upon men and women in a lower stratum of society. The Lord says concerning Him, "I have exalted one chosen out of the people" (Ps. 89:19). He is the people's Christ. He is a condescending Savior, who took little children up in His arms and blessed them and said, "Suffer the little children to come unto me, and forbid them not: for of such is the kingdom of God" (Mark 10:14). Notwithstanding all His glory and majesty, He disdains not the poor and needy, and His ear is ever open to the cry of the humble and contrite. He takes pity upon the prisoner, He hearkens to the wail of the sorrowful, He has respect for the broken in heart, and He is ever tender and compassionate to all who seek His aid. Surely this meekness of the Savior must commend the gospel to you.

The fourth wheel is *righteousness*. What a righteous Savior Jesus is, and what a righteous gospel His gospel is! A man might well fall in love with the gospel for this reason, if for no other, that it sets forth so clearly the majesty of divine justice. God determined to save sinners, yet He would not save them at the expense of justice. He delights in mercy, yet He would not indulge even His darling attribute to the detriment of His righteous law. Christ gave His back to the smiters and His cheeks to them that plucked off the hair; He hid not His face from shame and spitting. He yielded up His hands and His feet to the cruel nails, His body to pains indescribable, and His soul to agonies so terrible that He cried, "My soul is exceeding sorrowful unto death" (Mark 14:34). He bore "all that incarnate God could bear, with strength enough but none to spare," so that He might fully vindicate the justice of God. Righteousness well completed the number of the wheels of the chariot of salvation; may they, by His grace, draw it just where you are, and may that same grace constrain you to enter that chariot that you may ride in it to glory everlasting!

But a gospel chariot without Christ is like a chariot without a rider in it, and of what avail is an empty chariot? In the front of the chariot of the gospel stands Jesus Christ in all His glory and His majesty. I wish that all preachers would always recall this. Some of them seem to preach the doctrine of salvation, and others of them proclaim its precepts, and in that way they bring out the chariot, but there is no rider in it; they have left out the Christ who is its chief, indeed, its only glory. But whatever else the preacher may forget, he should never forget his Master but always give Him His rightful place. He should say to His Lord as the psalmist said to Jerusalem, "If I forget thee, O Jerusalem, let my right hand forget her cunning. If I do not remember thee, let my tongue cleave to the roof of my mouth" (Ps. 137:5–6). What is there for any man to preach about if he leave Jesus Christ out of his sermons? A teaching without Christ in it is a delusion and a sham, mere playing with immortal souls, a mockery both of God and of man. Jesus Christ and Him crucified should be the Alpha and the Omega of every sermon. In the chariot of our ministry I hope that we can without hesitation say that Jesus Christ rides in His glory and in His majesty.

But although Christ may thus ride in the chariot of our teaching, He must always be there in His omnipotent might and in the power of the ever-blessed Spirit. I want you who love Him to pray the psalmist's prayer: "Gird thy sword upon thy thigh, O most mighty, with thy glory and thy majesty. And in thy majesty ride prosperously because of truth and meekness and righteousness." There is a fine old Welsh hymn that I wish I could turn into English without spoiling it; it runs somewhat to this effect: "O Jesus, come forth! Leave the ivory palaces! Thy chariot waits for thee; come forth, come forth! Hell trembles before thee, all heaven adores thee, earth owns thy sway, men's hearts cannot resist thee; come forth, come forth! Bars of brass thou breakest, gates of iron give way before thee; come forth, come forth, O Jesus, for thy chariot awaits thee now!"

The Victory Won

"Thy right hand shall teach thee terrible things. Thine arrows are sharp in the heart of the king's enemies; whereby the people fall under thee." Many representations of Eastern monarchs picture them not only as wearing a sword upon the thigh when riding in the great war chariot but also as bearing a battle bow. The artists, wishing to flatter their royal masters, represented the king's arrows as going right through the hearts of the king's enemies. Our almighty Warrior has a sure aim; He never misses the heart at which He shoots His arrows. That same gospel that is like a two-edged sword is, in another aspect, like sharp arrows shot from the bow of a mighty archer. Arrows, you know, can do nothing until they are shot. The arrow is useless without the bow, and the bow itself is useless without the hand and arm of the man who bends it and speeds the arrow to the mark he wants to hit. It used to be said of William the Conqueror that no man in England except himself could bend his bow, and so is it with the bow that belongs to our great Conqueror. When He fits the arrows to the string and draws the bow with His almighty hand, the missile flies with irresistible force and buries itself in the heart at which the King took such unerring aim.

I take it that these arrows are intended to represent not so much the whole Bible as certain texts out of the Bible—*sharp arrows from the quiver of revelation*. Sometimes one arrow will be shot, and sometimes another, but they are all sharp. Have you ever felt the pang that goes through the heart when one of these sharp arrows strikes it? So long as it lasts, there is no pain so keen as that produced by conviction of sin, and there is no cure for that pain except from that very hand that shot the arrow that caused it.

These arrows are spoken of in the plural because, while there are arrows of conviction, arrows of justice, arrows of terror, there are also arrows of mercy, arrows of consolation. Where there are arrows that kill sin, there are also arrows that kill despair, which also is a sin. And as there are arrows that smite and slay our carnal hopes, so there are other arrows that effectually destroy our sinful fear. All these arrows are sharp in the heart of the King's enemies; there is no blunt one in the whole quiver.

Notice that *all these arrows belong to the King.* It is to the "most mighty" that the psalmist says, *"Thine* arrows." The truth never comes home to our heart and conscience until the Holy Spirit convinces us that it is God's truth. There are some doctrines in the Scriptures that many are unwilling to accept as divine although they are very clearly revealed in the Word, and they are truths that God has over and over again blessed to the salvation of souls. People have often said that the doctrine of election should not be preached lest it should prove to be a stumbling block in the way of sinners coming to Christ, yet I can testify that we have had scores of people in our church come to the Savior through sermons upon election, predestination, and those other great truths in which many of us believe and rejoice. They certainly are among the sharp arrows of our King.

Observe, too, *where the King's arrows go.* They all pierce the heart: "Thine arrows are sharp in the heart of the king's enemies." An arrow that strikes a person in the head would kill the person, but the King's arrows, when they merely strike the intellect by way of an assent to the truth of the gospel, are not effective as they are when they enter the heart. An arrow to the leg may cause you to limp upstairs to pray, but there has been no such killing work as there is when the King's arrows pierce the heart. When they strike there, they inflict a mortal wound, for out of the heart are the issues of life. O Lord, smite the heart! Kill the old life and give us new life. Slay the old man as Your enemy, but cause the new man to come forth as Your friend. Shoot Your arrows right through the heart that loves sin and hates You, the heart that loves drunkenness, that loves lust, that loves evil in any form. Kill that heart O Lord, and then give a new heart and a new spirit!

Let me remind you that there is a time coming when Christ will go forth to war with all His armor on; that is the time of which we read in the Revelation: "And out of his mouth goeth a sharp sword, that with it he should smite the nations: and he shall rule them with a rod of iron.... in righteousness he doth judge and make war" (Rev. 19:15, 11). It will be a terrible thing for all who are the enemies of the King in that day; His arrows will indeed be swift and sharp to slay. Do not long for that day to come if you are unconverted, for to you it will be a day of darkness. It will be a dreadful day for those who have despised and rejected the Christ of God when He shall fit His sharp arrows to the string, draw the bow, and pierce you to the heart. Where will you flee from the glance of His all-seeing eye? Up to the loftiest mountains His shafts shall fly after you; in the trackless deserts, in the densest forest, far out upon the mighty ocean, His arrows shall find you out. Try not to fly from Him, but flee to Him now. If a man wanted to shoot me with a bow and arrow, I would try to clasp him in my arms and hold him to my heart, for how could he shoot me then? Close in with Christ in this manner; run not from Him but run to Him, and clasp Him in your heart, and never let Him go.

If you yield to Christ, you will find that He will no longer be angry with you. He is loving and gracious, and He delights to welcome to His heart those who repent. He will receive you if you only trust Him, and then you will see him riding in His chariot in quite another fashion. Perhaps at first you will be afraid of Him and ask, "Lord, what have you come to do?" and He will reply, "I have come to strike your sins with my sharp arrows." One after another He will fit them to His bow and shoot at all He means to slay. He will kill your profanity, He will kill your pride, He will kill your self-righteousness—all of those will be pierced through and through by His unerring darts. He will shoot your self-trust and kill it outright and make you humble as a little child. He will shoot at your love of the world, at all your pleasures that are not holy pleasures, at every lust and every evil propensity within you, and down they will fall, every one slain by His sharp arrows. Blessed will it be for you when they are all slain, for who would wish to spare any of the King's enemies? Rather rise up yourself and help the King to slay them; surely you give no consideration to those who are your foes as well as His.

Trust the Savior. He died for sinners, bearing their sin in His own body on the tree. He died for all who trust Him, and they who trust Him shall find Him faithful and true, and He shall bring them home to His Father's house to dwell with Him forever. Oh, that all of us might be in that blessed company!

The metaphor of keys is intended, no doubt, to set forth the double thought of our Lord's possessing both the rightful and the actual dominion over death and hell. The rightful dominion, I say, for often it has been the custom to present the keys of cities to honorary dignitaries in formal state, recognizing that the person's majesty was the lawful owner and rightful sovereign of the city. So Christ has the keys of death and hell—He is rightfully the Lord over those dark regions and rules them by indefeasible title of sovereignty. But in commonest life, the key is associated with actual possession and power. When the tenant gives up the key to the landlord, the owner has the house again under his power and in his possession by that act and deed. So Christ actually rules and manages in all the matters of the grave and overrules all the councils of hell, restraining the mischievous devices of Satan or turning them to subserve His own designs of good. Our Lord Jesus Christ still is supreme. His kingdom, willingly or unwillingly, extends over all existences in whatever regions they may be.

Chapter Two

Christ with the
Keys of Death and Hell

I am he that liveth, and was dead; and, behold, I am alive for evermore, Amen; and have the keys of hell and of death
—Revelation 1:18.

DEATH IS A LAND OF DARKNESS, as darkness itself, without any order, yet a sovereign eye surveys it, and a master hand holds its key. Hell also is a horrible region, where powers of evil and of terror hold their high court and dread assembly; but hell trembles at the presence of the Lord, and there is a throne higher than the throne of evil. Let us rejoice that nothing in heaven or on earth or in places under the earth is left to itself to create anarchy. Everywhere, serene above the floods, the Lord sits as King forever and ever. No province of the universe is free from the divine rule. Things do not come by chance. Nowhere do chance and chaos reign, nowhere is evil really and permanently enthroned. Rest assured that the Lord has prepared His throne in the heavens and His kingdom rules over all, for if the lower hell and death are subject to His government, much more all things that are on this lower world.

From Revelation 1 we observe that the government of hell and of death is vested in the person of the man Christ Jesus. He who holds the keys to these dreadful regions is described as "one like unto the Son of man"(vs. 13), and we know that He was our Lord

Jesus Christ Himself. John saw a strange and glorious change in Him but still recognized the old likeness, perhaps impressed by the nail prints and other marks of manhood that he had seen in Him while He was in the days of His flesh. What an honor is thus conferred upon mankind! Unto which of the angels said He at any time, "Thou shalt bear the keys of hell and of death"? Yet these keys are committed to the Son of man, bone of our bone and flesh of our flesh, made in all points like unto His brethren and rules over all. Yet manhood is not so exalted as of itself and apart from Godhead, for while the description given of our Lord by John as he saw Him at Patmos is evidently human, yet is He is also convincingly divine. There is a glow of glory about that mysterious manhood that stood between the golden candlesticks, that is a light apart, belonging only to the everlasting God, whose Son the Redeemer is and whose equal He counts it not robbery to be. Jesus is in essence "who is over all, God blessed for ever" (Rom. 9:5). Let us rejoice, then, in the condescension of God in taking man into such union with Godhead that now in the person of Christ, man has dominion over all the works of God's hands; and not only does He rule over all sheep and oxen and the fowl of the air and whatever passes through the paths of the sea, but also death and Hades are committed to the dominion of the glorified man. "That at the name of Jesus every knee should bow, of things in heaven, and things in earth, and things under the earth; and that every tongue should confess that Jesus Christ is Lord, to the glory of God the Father" (Phil. 2:10–11).

The metaphor of keys is intended, no doubt, to set forth the double thought of our Lord's possessing both the rightful and the actual dominion over death and hell. The rightful dominion, I say, for often it has been the custom to present the keys of cities to honorary dignitaries in formal state, recognizing that the person's majesty was the lawful owner and rightful sovereign of the city. So Christ has the keys of death and hell—He is rightfully the Lord over those dark regions and rules them by indefeasible title of sovereignty. But in commonest life, the key is associated with actual possession and power. When the tenant gives up the key to the landlord, the owner has the house again under his power and in his possession by that act and deed. So Christ actually rules and manages in all the matters of the grave and overrules all the councils of hell, restraining the mischievous devices of Satan or turning them to subserve His own designs of good. Our Lord Jesus Christ still is supreme. His kingdom, willingly or unwillingly, extends over all existences in whatever regions they may be.

It may be well to mention that the word translated *hell*, though it may be rightfully referred to the region of lost and damned spirits, need not be restricted to that. The word is *Hades*, which signifies the dwelling place of spirits, and so it may include both heaven and hell; no doubt it does include them both in many places and, I think, in this verse. Our Lord, then, has the keys of heaven and hell and death. Wherever separate spirits are not existing, Christ is King, and over the iron gate through which men pass into the disembodied state, the authority of Christ is paramount. All hail! You brightness of the Father's glory, may You forevermore be adored!

The Power of These Keys

A key is first of all used *for opening*, and hence our Lord can open the gates of death and hell. It is His to open the gate of the separated spirits, to admit His saints one by one to their eternal felicity. When the time shall come for us to depart out of this world to the Father, no hand but that of the beloved Son shall put that golden key into the lock and open the pearly gate that admits the righteous to the spirit-land. When we have waited awhile as disembodied spirits in Paradise, it will be Christ's work to open the gates of the grave wherein our bodies shall have been confined so that at the trump of the archangel we may rise to immortality. He is the resurrection and the life; because He lives, we shall live also. At His command every bolt of death's prison house shall be drawn, and the huge iron gates of the sepulchers shall be rolled back. Then shall the body sown in weakness be raised in power, sown in dishonor be raised in glory.

We need not ask the question, "Can these dry bones live?" when we see in the hands of our omnipotent Savior the golden key. Death in vain shall have gathered up the carcasses of millions of his treasure, but Jesus shall loose all these treasures in a moment. Of all that the Father gave to Christ, He will lose nothing but will surely raise it up at the last day. Christ has purchased the bodies as well as the souls of His people; rest assured that He will not lose a part of what He has redeemed by blood. It is not the Father's will that the Redeemer should be defrauded of any part of His purchased possession. "Thy dead men shall live, together with my dead body shall they arise" (Isa. 26:19).

But a key is also used *to shut* the door, and even so Jesus will both shut in and shut out. His golden key will shut His people into heaven, as Noah was shut in the ark. There is no fear that glorified saints shall fall from their high estate or that they shall perish after all the salvation that they have experienced. Heaven is the place of eternal safety. There the gates shall be fast shut by which their foes could enter or by which their joys could leave them. But there is the dark side of this shutting of the gate. It is Christ who, with His key, shall shut the gates of heaven against unbelievers. When the Master has once shut the doors to heaven, it will be useless for mere professors to come with anxious knock and bitter cry, "Lord, open to us." Once the Son of David closes mercy's gate upon the soul of a man, the iron bar shall never be raised again. It will be terrible to find yourself thrust forth into "outer darkness; there shall be weeping and gnashing of teeth" (Matt. 22:13). Jesus, with His sovereign key, has locked out of heaven all sinners who die unrepentant and shut out of heaven all sin; shut out of heaven all temptations, all trouble, and all pain and death; shut out of heaven all the temptations of the devil, and not even the howling of that dog of hell shall be heard across the jasper walls of that New Jerusalem.

A key is also used to shut in, in reference to hell, those spirits who are confined there. "Between us and you," Abraham said to the rich man in hell, "there is a great gulf fixed: so that they which would pass from hence to you cannot; neither can they pass to us, that would come from thence" (Luke 16:26). It is Christ's key that has shut in the lost spirits, so that they cannot roam by way of respite or escape by way of pardon. May you never be so shut in. Christ has the key by which He shuts in Satan. Satan is to be bound for a thousand years, but Jesus shall hold the chain, for only our Emmanuel could bind this old dragon. When temptation is kept away from a Christian, it is the Savior's restraining power that holds back the enemy; and if the enemy comes in like a flood, it is by permission of Jesus that the trial comes. The key that shall bind the old dragon in those blessed days of millennial rest is in our Lord's power, and the final triumph, when no sin shall any further be known on earth and evil shall be pent up in the grim caverns of hell, will be achieved by Christ Jesus, our Lord and God. To open, then, and to shut out, to shut in and to shut out, these are the work of the keys.

By the keys we must further understand that our Lord *rules*, for the key is an Eastern metaphor for government. He shall have the key of David: "the government shall be upon his shoulder" (Isa. 9:6). We understand by Christ's having the keys of hell that He *rules over the damned spirits*. These spirits would not in this life have this Man to rule over them, but in the life to come they must submit whether they will to or not. In that seething caldron, every wave of fire is guided by the will of the Man Christ, and the mark of His sovereignty is on every iron chain. This the ungodly will be compelled to feel with terror, for although the ferocity of their natures will remain, the boastfulness of their pride shall be taken from them. Though they would still revolt, they shall find themselves hopelessly fettered and powerless to accomplish their designs. Though they yearn to continue stouthearted with Pharaoh and cry, "Who is the LORD, that I should obey his voice?" (Exod. 5:2), they shall find themselves like Belshazzar on that dreadful night when his city was destroyed; they shall wring their hands in anguish and bite their tongues in despair.

One of the great terrors of the lost in hell will be this, that He who came to save was rejected by them and now only reveals Himself to them as mighty to destroy. He who held out the silver scepter when they would not touch it shall forever break them with a rod of iron for their willful impenitence. What must be the consternation of those who were loudest against Christ on earth, the men who denied His deity, those who vented curses upon His blessed name, who were never satisfied unless they uttered bitter words against the man of Nazareth! What will be their amazement! What confusion shall overwhelm the man who said he lived in the twilight of Christianity, to find himself where the blaze of Christ's glory shall forever be as a furnace to his guilty soul! "Kiss the Son, lest he be angry, and ye perish from the way, when his wrath is kindled but a little. Blessed are all they that put their trust in him" (Ps. 2:12).

As in hell Christ has power over all the damned spirits, so our text implies that He has power over all *the devils*. It was willfulness, doubtless, that made Satan revolt against God. Perhaps Milton's poetic surmise is not far from the truth, and Satan did think it "better to rule in hell than serve in heaven." But, fool that he was, he has to serve in hell with a service ten thousand times more irksome than that which would have been his lot in heaven. There, firstborn son of the morning, brightest of the angels of God, how happy might have been his perpetual service of the Most High. But now blighted by the scathing thunderbolts of Jehovah, he crawls forth from his den degraded, going like a serpent on his belly, debased beneath the very beasts of the field, seeking to tempt others that they may come into the same loathsome condition with himself. Yet note how even in those temptations of his, Satan is ruled by Christ! Jesus permits the foul fiend to tempt, but there is always a limit. "Only upon himself put not forth thine hand" (Job 1:12) was Satan's limit regarding Job, but beyond that point he must not heap up the patriarch's agony; thus, in all cases Christ rules Satan by restraining him.

Even in that which Satan is permitted to do, God strengthens His servants so that Satan gets no honor in the contest but retires continually more and more disgraced by being defeated by the poor sons of Adam. Cunning spirit as he is, he is beaten in the conflict with poor creatures who dwell in flesh. And better still, out of all the temptations of Satan, God's people are made to derive profit and strength. In our conflicts, we are taught our weakness and led to fly to Christ for strength. An abject slave of Christ are you, O Satan; a very scullion in the kitchen of providence. When you think most to effect your own purposes and to overthrow the kingdom of Christ on earth, even then what are you but a mere hack, accomplishing still the purposes of your Master, whom in vain you blaspheme! Lo, at Christ's side are the keys of hell. Let the whole legion of accursed spirits tremble.

I have said that the word *Hades* may include hell and heaven or the whole state of separated spirits. Hence, we are bound to say that our Savior rules over all *the glorified spirits* in heaven and all the angels that are their associates and ministering spirits. Is this not a delightful reflection that the Redeemer is the King of angels, for in times of danger He can send an angel to strengthen us, or, if needs be, twenty legions of angels would soon find their way to stand side by side with the weak but faithful warrior of the cross. Believer, you can never be cast where divine comfort cannot reach you. Angels see their way by night and journey over mount and sea with unwearied flight, unimpeded by wind or tempest. They can meet your enemy, the prince of the power of the air, and overcome him for you. And doubtless they have often done so when we were unaware of it. You shall never be left to perish, when the chariots of

God that are twenty thousand, even thousands of angels, are all at the beck and command of Him who has redeemed you with His precious blood.

Joyous is the thought that Jesus rules over all redeemed spirits in heaven, for we hope to be there soon, and this shall be among our dearest joys that without temptation, without weakness, without weariness, we shall serve our Lord day and night in His temple. Of all the joys of heaven, next to that of being with Christ, one delights to think of serving Christ. How rapturous will be our song! How zealously we will praise Him! How sincere will be our service! If He should give us commissions to distant worlds, as perhaps He will; if He shall prepare us to become preachers of His truth to creatures in unknown orbs; if He shall call us through revolving ages to publish to new created myriads the wondrous grace of God in Christ, with what ardent pleasure will we accept the service! How constantly, how heartily will we tell out the story of our salvation by the precious blood of Jesus! Oh, that we could serve Him here as we wish, but we shall serve Him there without fault or flaw. Oh, happy heaven, because Jesus has the key of it and reigns supreme, when shall we stand upon the sea of glass before His throne?

Our Lord is said to have the keys of death, from which we gather that *all the matters of death* are at His disposal alone. No man can die unless Jesus opens the mystic door of death. Even the ungodly man owes his spared life to Christ. It is the intercession and intervention of Jesus that keeps breath even in the swearer's nostrils. Long since had you been consumed in the fire of God's wrath, had not Jesus used His authority to keep you out of the jaws of death. As for His saints, it is their consolation that their death is entirely in His hands. In the midst of disease and war, we shall never die until He wills it; in the times of the greatest healthiness, we shall not live a second longer than Jesus has purposed. The place, the circumstance, the exact second of our departure have all been appointed by Him and settled long ago in love and wisdom. A thousand angels could not hurl us to the grave, nor could a host of cherubim confine us there one moment after Jesus said, "Arise." This is our comfort. We are "immortal until our work is done." Let us never fear death, then, but rather rejoice at the approach of it, since it comes at our dear Bridegroom's bidding. "For to me to live is Christ, and to die is gain" (Phil. 1:21). Though the prospect of our

Lord's coming is sweet, immeasurably sweet, yet the prospect of going to Him meanwhile if He so wills it is not without its sweetness, too. Christ has the key of death, and therefore death to us is no longer a gate of terror.

The Key of Power

Where did Christ obtain this right to have the keys of hell and death? Does He not derive it first of all from *His Godhead*? When He says, "I am he that liveth," this is language that only God can use, for while we live, yet it is only with a borrowed life, like the moon that shines with a borrowed light; and as the moon cannot say, "I am the shining sphere," neither can man say, "I am he that liveth." Jesus being God claims the self-existence and can say, "I am he that liveth." He certainly has power over heaven and earth and hell. There can be no dispute concerning the divine prerogative. He is the Creator of all things; He is the Preserver of all things; all power belongs to Him. As for all things that are apart from Him, they would vanish as a puff of air is gone if He willed it. He alone exists, He alone is; therefore, let Him wear the crown, let Him have undivided rule.

That doctrine of the deity of Christ, how I tremble for those who will not receive it! If there is anything in the Word of God that is clear and plain, it is surely this. If there is anything that can give us comfort when we come to rest upon Christ, it is just this, that we are not looking to an angel or depending upon a creature but are resting upon Him who is Alpha and Omega, the beginning and the end, the Almighty God. Having such a rock of our salvation as the ever-living and ever-blessed God, let the thought kindle in our souls the purest joy.

The key to this power lies also in our Savior's *conquests*. He has the keys of death and hell because He has actually conquered both these powers. You know how He met hell in the dreadful onset in the garden of Gethsemane, how all the powers of darkness there combined against Him. Such was the agony of that struggle that He sweat great drops of blood falling to the ground, yet He sustained the brunt of that onset without wavering and kept the field unbeaten. He continued still to wrestle with those evil powers upon the cross, and in that thick midday-midnight into which no curious eyes could pry, in the midst of that darkness He continued still to fight, His heel bruised but breaking meanwhile the dragon's head. Grim was the contest, but glorious was the victory, worthy to be sung by angels in eternal chorus. Take down your sweetest harps you seraphs, lift up your loudest notes, you cherubim, to Him who fought the dragon and overcame him, to Him be glory forever and ever. Well does Jesus deserve to rule the provinces that He has subdued in fight. He has conquered the king of hell and destroyed the works of the devil, and He has the sovereign right to be King over the domain of the vanquished.

As to death, you know how our Lord vanquished him! By death He conquered death. When the hands were nailed, they become potent to fight with the grave; when the feet were fastened to the wood, then began they to trample on the sepulcher; when the death pangs began to thrill through every nerve of the Redeemer's body, then His arrows shot through the loins of death; and when His anguished soul was ready to take its speedy flight and leave His blessed corpse, then did the tyrant sustain a mortal wound. Our Lord's entrance into the tomb was the taking possession of His enemies' stronghold; His sleep within the sepulcher's stony walls was the transformation of the prison into a couch of rest. But especially in the resurrection when, because He could not be held by the bonds of death, neither could His soul be kept in Hades, He rose again in glory, then did He become the "death of death and hell's destruction," and rightfully was He acknowledged the plague of death and the destruction of the grave.

Whether, when our Lord died, His soul actually descended into hell itself we will not assert or deny. I leave that to the theologians to debate. It is not for us to speak where the Scripture is silent, but may it not be true that the Great Conqueror cast the shadow of His presence over the dens of His enemies as He passed in triumph by the gates of hell? May not the keepers of that infernal gate have seen His star and trembled as they also beheld their master like lightning fall from heaven? Would it not add to His glory if those who were His implacable foes were made to know of His complete triumph? At any rate, it was but a passing presence, for we know that swiftly He sped to the gates of heaven, taking with Him the repentant thief to be with Him that day in Paradise. Jesus had opened thus the grave by going into it, hell by passing by it, heaven by passing into it, heaven again by passing out of it, death again by rising from it into this world, and heaven by His ascension. Thus passing and repassing, He has proved that the keys are at His side. By His achievements, by His doing, He has won for Himself the power of the keys.

We have one more truth to remember, that Jesus Christ is installed in this high place of power and dignity by the Father Himself as *a reward for what He has done*. He was Himself to "divide the spoil with the strong," but the Father had promised to give Him a "portion with the great" (Isa. 53:12). See the reward for the shame that He endured among the sons of men! He stooped lower than the lowest, He has risen higher than the highest; He wore the crown of thorns, but now He wears the triple crown of heaven and earth and hell. He was the servant of servants, but now He is King of kings and Lord of lords. Earth would not find Him a shelter, a stable must be the place of His birth, and a borrowed tomb the sepulcher of His dead body. But now, all space is His, time and eternity tremble at His bidding, and there is no creature, however minute or vast, that is not subject to Him. How greatly has the Father glorified Him whom men rejected and despised! Let us adore Him; let our hearts, while we think over these plain and precious truths, come and spread their riches at His feet and crown Him Lord of all.

Therefore, "Fear Not"

This manifestation of Christ as having the keys of death and hell was given to the trembling John, who had fallen down with astonishment and dread as one dead. To comfort him, and as if to make this clear, the words were spoken in the preceding verse, "Fear not." I address those same words to you. "Fear not." Why fear? There is no possible cause for fear for believers, since Jesus lives. If poverty comes, can you be poor in Christ? If sickness comes, "the LORD will strengthen him upon the bed of languishing: thou wilt make all his bed in his sickness" (Ps. 41:3); and since Christ is with you, sickness shall work your soul's health. In temptation, Christ will pray for you that your faith does not fail, though Satan has desired to sift you like wheat. Should frailty come, you fear that some dark hour may overcome your faith. Yet you are one with Him who ever lives, and who can possibly destroy you while the vital energy pours from your covenant Head into you as a member of His body?

I say again, there is no possible cause for fear to any soul who believes in Christ. You shall ransack the corruptions of your heart within, you shall count your trials without, you shall imagine all the tribulations that shall come tomorrow, you shall reflect on all the sins that were with you yesterday and in the past, you shall peer into the shades of death and horrors of hell; but I declare solemnly to you that there is nothing in any of these that you, believing in Christ, have any cause to fear. If they all should unite, if the whole together, the world, the flesh, the devil, if a trinity of malice should all come against you while you have a living faith in the living Savior, "Fear not" is but the logical inference from that precious fact. Carry this fearlessness in your life and be happy as a king. Oh, with nothing else but a living Savior, how rich should a saint to be! And with everything else, but missing that living Savior, how miserable the richest and the greatest of men always would be if they did but know their true state as before the Lord!

Observe that this "Fear not" may be specially applied to the matter of the grave. We need not fear to die, because Jesus has the key of the grave. We shall never pass through that iron gate with an angel to be our conductor or some grim executioner to lead us, as it were, into a dreary place of hideous imprisonment. No, Jesus shall come to our dying bed, in all the glory of His supernal splendor, and shall say, "Come away with Me." The sight of Jesus as He thrusts in the key and opens that gate of death shall make you forget the supposed terrors of the grave, for they are but superstitions and suppositions, and you shall find it sweet to die. Never fear death again. Your dying hour will be the best hour you have ever known, your last will be your richest moment. It shall be the beginning of heaven, the rising of a sun that shall go no more down forever. Let the fear of death be banished from you by faith in a living Savior.

Some believers have a fear of the world of spirits. They say, "It must be a dreadful thing to enter that unknown land. We have stood and peered as best we could through the mist that gathers over the black river and have wondered what it must be like to have left the body and to be flitting, a naked soul, through that land from which no traveler has ever returned." But perhaps you imagined that you were sailing into an enemy's country, but Jesus is the King of Hades as well as Lord of earth. You do but pass from one province of your Lord's empire into another and indeed from a darker into a brighter territory of the same one sovereign. In that spirit-land they speak the same tongue, the tongue of the New Jerusalem, that you have already begun to lisp; they own the King whom you here obey; and when you shall enter into the assemblies of those disembodied spirits you shall find them all singing in the praise of the same glorious One whom you have adored, rejoicing in His light that was your light on earth and triumphing in His love that was your Savior here below. Be of good courage, Jesus is King of Hades. Fear not.

Neither fear the devil. We must be watchful against him, but we must not fear him so that he may get an advantage from our fear. "Resist the devil, and he will flee from you" (James 4:7). Stand trembling, and he will attack you worse than ever. The boldness of courageous faith is that which makes the devil tremble. Well may you be brave, for when he comes howling at you like a lion, you may taunt him thus and say, "Show your teeth and howl and yell, but you are chained. You cannot do more than threaten me. You think to worry me, but you cannot devour me, and therefore I defy you. Be gone, in the name of Jesus Christ who bruised you, dragon of hell, be gone!" The courage that shall enable you to thus deal with the enemy shall give you a rapid victory. He is a chained enemy; this leviathan has a bit between his jaws and a hook in his nose. He may trouble you, but you shall be "more than conquerors through him that loved us" (Rom. 8:37).

One other word to the believer. Should not this lofty theme lead us to worship Him who has the keys? Let us come into His presence with thanksgiving and show ourselves glad in Him with songs. Preaching is not the great purpose of going to church, listening to sermons is not the great aim. The end is to glorify God in service, and especially in the singing of His praises. Worship rendered to God in prayer and praise is the true fruit. Never miss an opportunity to extol Him with your praises and to honor Him with the holiness of your lives and the zeal of your service. Is He King over heaven and death and hell? Then shall He be King over the triple territory of my spirit, soul, and body, and I will make all my powers and passions yield Him praise.

What would it be to you today if the gates of death were opened to you? I implore you to listen to His gospel. Trust implicitly in Him who died on the cross of Calvary to make atonement for your sins. Trust in Him, and then come forth and confess your trust. Be baptized in His name, confessing your sins, and acknowledge yourself to be His disciple. This is the gospel: reject it at your peril. Submit to it, I beseech you, for Christ's sake.

But now in the passage before us a door was opened to heaven, and that disciple whom Jesus loved saw what he had never seen—what he had never imagined. He saw the same warrior Lord, but after quite another fashion. If John had continued to look with the eye of sense at Christ and His followers even to this day and had viewed the battle as it is to be seen in history upon earth, he would have said that he saw the same despised and rejected One at the head of a band equally despised and rejected, leading them to prison and death. He would have told you how this very day the banner of the gospel is borne aloft amid smoke and fire, and Christ crucified is proclaimed amid contention and ridicule. He would have drawn in black colors the scene of the battle, the great battle that is raging among the sons of men at this very hour. But now a door was opened in heaven, and John saw the scene as God sees it. He looked upon it from heaven's perspective and saw the conflict between good and evil, between Christ and Satan, between truth and error; he saw it in heaven's own clear view, and he then wrote the vision that we also might see it. If we are sharers in this conflict, if we are following the Lamb wherever He goes, if we are pledged to the truth and to the right, if we are sworn to the precious blood of atonement and to the grand doctrines of the gospel, it will do us good and stir our blood to stand on one of the serene hilltops of heaven above the mists of earth and look upon the battle that rages still upon the earth and will rage on till Armageddon shall conclude the war. If we can behold the scene, God strengthening our eyes, it may strengthen our hands for the conflict, our hearts for the fight.

Chapter Three

The Rider on the White Horse

And I saw heaven opened, and behold a white horse; and he that sat upon him was called Faithful and True, and in righteousness he doth judge and make war. His eyes were as a flame of fire, and on his head were many crowns; and he had a name written, that no man knew, but he himself. And he was clothed with a vesture dipped in blood: and his name is called The Word of God. And the armies which were in heaven followed him upon white horses, clothed in fine linen, white and clean. And out of his mouth goeth a sharp sword, that with it he should smite the nations: and he shall rule them with a rod of iron: and he treadeth the winepress of the fierceness and wrath of Almighty God. And he hath on his vesture and on his thigh a name written, KING OF KINGS, AND LORD OF LORDS—Revelation 19:11–16.

THE BELOVED JOHN was, above all other men, familiar with the humble Savior. John had leaned his head upon His bosom and knew better than any of the other apostles the painful beatings of his Lord's sorrowful heart. Never from his mind could be erased the likeness of Christ, the visage more marred than that of any man. He had seen the dear sufferer on that dreadful night when He was covered with bloody sweat in Gethsemane; He had seen Him after He had been beaten and scourged in Herod's palace and Pilate's hall; He had even stood at the foot of the cross and seen his divine master in the extreme agonies of death; and therefore the tender, affectionate heart of John would never permit his Master's suffering image to fade from his memory. Truly, if he had spoken to us in vision—in symbolic terms—concerning what he had seen of his Lord and Master here below, he would have described Him as a footman going forth to fight alone, with no armies following Him, for all His disciples forsook Him and fled, Himself wearing no glittering armor but His garments dipped in blood and His face smeared with shame. John would have told you how the solitary Champion fought alone amid the dust and smother of the battle and how He fell and bit the dust, so that His foe set his evil foot upon Him and for a moment rejoiced over Him. He would have told you how He leaped again from the grave and trod down His adversaries and led captivity captive. Such would have been, only in far nobler terms, John's description of his first sight of his wrestling warrior Lord.

But now in the passage before us a door was opened to heaven, and that disciple whom Jesus loved saw what he had never seen— what he had never imagined. He saw the same warrior Lord, but after quite another fashion. If John had continued to look with the eye of sense at Christ and His followers even to this day and had viewed the battle as it is to be seen in history upon earth, he would have said that he saw the same despised and rejected One at the head of a band equally despised and rejected, leading them to prison and death. He would have told you how this very day the banner of the gospel is borne aloft amid smoke and fire, and Christ crucified is proclaimed amid contention and ridicule. He would have drawn in black colors the scene of the battle, the great battle that is raging among the sons of men at this very hour. But now a door was opened in heaven, and John saw the scene *as God sees it*. He looked upon it from heaven's perspective and saw the conflict between good and evil, between Christ and Satan, between truth and error; he saw it in heaven's own clear view, and he then wrote the vision that we also might see it. If we are sharers in this conflict, if we are following the Lamb wherever He goes, if we are pledged to the truth and to the right, if we are sworn to the precious blood of atonement and to the grand doctrines of the gospel, it will do us good and stir our blood to stand on one of the serene hilltops of heaven above the mists of earth and look upon the battle that rages still upon the earth and will rage on till Armageddon shall conclude the war. If we can behold the scene, God strengthening our eyes, it may strengthen our hands for the conflict, our hearts for the fight.

John Saw Our Captain

Let us notice John's glorious state. He says, "I saw heaven opened, and behold a white horse; and he that sat upon him." While Jesus was here, as we have already said, He was a foot soldier; He had to plunge through mire and dirt and walk as wearily as any of the rest of the warrior company. But now that He has ascended, though He continues still to fight, it is after another manner. Of course, the terms are symbolic, but our Lord is here described as sitting upon a gallant steed, charging His foes upon a snow-white horse. This means that Christ is *honored* now. He is no weary, dusty, fainting footman now, I promise you. Time was when Solomon said that he saw servants upon horses and princes walking in the dust, and so it was with Christ: Pilate and Herod rode the high horse, and Jesus must walk in pain and in dishonor. But now, like a greater Mordecai, He rides on the King's horse, for this is the man whom the King delights to honor. In royal state our Jesus goes forth to war, not as a common soldier but as a glorious prince, royally mounted.

By a horse is denoted not only honor but also *power*. To the Jews the use of the horse in warfare was unusual, so that when it was used by their adversaries, they imputed to it great force. Jesus Christ has a mighty power today, a power that none can measure. He was crucified in weakness, but where is the weakness now? He gave His hands to the nail and His feet to be fastened to the wood, but He does so no longer. Now has He mounted on the horse of His exceeding great power, and He rules in heaven and in earth, and none can stop His hand or put Him to dishonor or dispute His will. O you who love Him, feast your eyes upon Him this day. Gaze upon Him for yourself and let your eyes be filled with the image, as you see Him, once despised and rejected, now taking to Himself His great power.

Here is symbolized *swiftness* as well. Christ had to walk from city to city when He was here, hardly getting through them all till His time was accomplished, but now His word runs very swiftly. He has but to will it and the voice of His gospel is heard to the utmost ends of the earth; their line is gone out through all the earth, and their words to the end of the world. Everywhere is the gospel preached, and today is fulfilled before your eyes the words of the prophet Zechariah: "The LORD of hosts hath visited his flock the house of Judah, and hath made them as his goodly horse in the battle.... and they shall fight, because the LORD is with them" (Zech. 10:3, 5).

The color of the horse is meant to denote *victory*. The Roman conqueror, when he enjoyed a triumph on returning from a campaign, rode up the Via Sacra on a white horse, and the Romans crowded to the housetops to gaze upon the hero as he displayed his spoils. Now Jesus Christ is admired of angels and elect spirits, who throng the windows of heaven to gaze upon Him who is glorified by His Father. There is a pale horse, and his name that sits on him is Death, and there is a horse red with blood, and yet another black with judgment; but His is a white horse, significant of comfort and of joy to all who know and love Him. He comes to fight, but the fight is for peace; He comes to smite, but it is to smite His people's enemies; He comes as a conqueror, but it is as a delivering conqueror who scatters His flowers and roses where He rides, breaking only the oppressor but blessing the citizens whom He emancipates.

I seldom speak upon this theme, for it seems too great for me, but I would bid the saints of God who have wept at Gethsemane now lift up your eyes and smile as you see that same Redeemer who once lay agonizing beneath the olive trees now riding on the white horse. Your Lord at this moment is no more despised, but all the glory that heaven itself can devise is lavished upon Him.

John looked in the open vault of heaven, and he had time not only to see the horse but also to mark the character of Him who sat upon it. He says that He who sat upon the horse was *called Faithful and True*. By this you may know your Lord. He has been a faithful and true friend to you. O soldiers of the cross, when has He ever deceived you? When has He failed you or forgotten you? Faithful? Ah, that He is, faithful to every word that He has spoken. And true? Do you not recognize Him, for is He not the truth—the very truth of God? Has He not kept every promise that He has made you, and have you not found His teachings to be everlastingly settled upon divine veracity? And faithful and true has He been to the great Father. The work He undertook to do He has accomplished. He has in nothing drawn back from the covenant commitments under which He placed Himself of old. He stood as the surety of His people, and He has been faithful and true to that painful promise. He came to be the deliverer of His elect, and He has accomplished the deliverance. He has not turned either to the right hand or to the left, but He has been faithful and true to every pledge that He gave to His Father for the deliverance of His chosen.

Even His enemies, though they give Him many a foul word, cannot say that He is not faithful and true. He has not played false, even to the basest devil in hell, nor has He deceived in any respect the basest man who lives. Nor will He, for when the day comes to keep His word of terror, He will make the penalty tally to every syllable of the warning and mete out vengeance with a line and judgment with a plummet, and even His adversaries shall confess that His name is Faithful and True. They called Him many bad names when He was here; they said he had a devil and was crazy; but now it is acknowledged that His name is Faithful and True. *We* acknowledge it with intense delight and are glad to think that He leads the troops of heaven to the fight.

John still looked, and as he gazed with opened eye he marked *the mode of action and of warfare* that the champion used, for he says, "In righteousness he doth judge and make war." Jesus is the only king who always wars this way. There have been brilliant exceptions to the general rule, but war is usually as deceitful as it is bloody, and the words of diplomats are a heap of lies. It seems impossible that men should deliberate about peace and war without immediately forgetting the meaning of words and the bonds of honesty. War still seems to be a piece of business in which truth would be out of place; it is a matter so accursed that falsehood is there most at home, and righteousness retires from the plain. But as for our King, it is in righteousness that He judges and makes war. Christ's kingdom needs no deception: the plainest speech and the clearest truth—these are the weapons of our warfare. Jesus bids His champions to come forth with nothing but His Word and to speak that Word faithfully, as they receive it, whether men will hear it or not. He tells His people, wherever they are, to live righteously, soberly, and in all integrity, and He Himself shakes off, as a man shakes off a viper from his hand, anything that is contrary to truth and holiness. This is our champion, and I warrant you are as happy as I am that He sits on the white horse and has the upper hand. Since He fights in this manner, the more of such warfare, the better for mankind.

John, gazing still into the open door, saw a little—not much— of the person of His blessed Master. And, of course, he looked first into *those eyes*, those dear eyes that had so often been filled with tears and that at last were even red with weeping. John gazed into them, or wished to do so, but he had to cover his own eyes, for they were dazzled. John says, "His eyes were as a flame of fire." Think of your Master on the white horse with such eyes as these. Why are they like a flame of fire? Why, first, to discern the secrets of all hearts. There are no secrets here that Christ does not see. There is no lewd thought, no unbelieving skepticism, that Christ does not read. There is no hypocrisy, no formalism, no deceit, that He does not scan as easily as a man reads a page in a book. His eyes are like a flame of fire to read us through and through and to know us to our inmost soul. Those eyes like a flame of fire belong to our Champion that He may understand all the plots and crafts of all our foes. We are sometimes alarmed by spiritual deceit and the plots of infidelity that dive very low. But what does it matter? *His* eyes are like a flame of fire: He knows what they are about. He will confound their politics, He will expose their tricks, and still lead on His host conquering and to conquer. Let us never fear while He is on the white horse with such eyes as His.

It is natural that John should carry his glance from the eyes to *the brow*; and as he looked at our Champion on the white horse, he saw that on His head were many crowns. The last John had seen there was a crown of thorns, but that was gone; and in the place of the once crown of the briars of the earth he saw many crowns of the jewels of heaven. There rests the crown of creation, for this Word made heaven and earth; the crown of providence, for this man now rules the nations with a rod of iron; the crown of grace, for it is from His royal hand that blessings are bestowed; the crown of the Church, for be it known to all men that there is no head of the Church but Christ, and woe to those who steal the title. He is head over all things to His Church, and King in the midst of her. Yes, on His head are many crowns placed there by individual souls that He has saved. We have each one tried to crown Him in our poor way, and we will still do so as long as we live. All power is given to Him in heaven and in earth, and therefore well may multitudes of diadems adorn that august brow that once was belted with thorns. Glory be to the Son of God! Our hearts adore You!

Looking at Him, John saw one more thing, namely, *His vesture*. John says that His vesture was dipped in blood. Oh, but this is the grandest thought about our Master wherever He may be, that He is ever a man wearing the bloody garment. As the atoning sacrifice, He is at His best. We love Him as we see the white lily of His perfect nature, but the rose of Sharon is the flower for us, for its sweet perfume breathes life to our fainting souls. Yes, He bled, and this is the greatest thing we can say of Him. His life was glorious, but His death transcends it. A living Christ, a reigning Christ—we are charmed as we think of this; but oh, the bleeding Christ, the bleeding Christ is for me! As the blood is the life, so is His blood life to us—the life of the gospel, the life of our hopes. One delights to think of Him who, though He rides the white horse, has never taken off the bloody shirt in which He won our redemption. He looks like a Lamb that has been slain and wears His priesthood still. Whenever He goes to conquer, it is with this vesture dipped in blood. Oh, preach Him, you His servants, preach Him in His bloodred vesture. You shall never see souls saved if you portray Him in any other type of coat. You take His own garment from Him and put on that of another, and you pretend that you are making Him illustrious as you put on Him a scarlet robe. But His own blood is His beauty and His triumph. Let Him come before us in that, and our hearts shall crown Him with loudest acclaim.

One other thing John saw, and that was *His name.* But here John seems to contradict himself. He says that He had a name that no man knows, yet he says that His name was the Word of God. Oh, but it is all true, for in such a one as our Master there must be paradoxes. No man knows His name. None of us know all His nature. His loves passes our knowledge. His goodness, His majesty, His humiliation, His glory, all these transcend your understanding. You cannot know Him to the depths! If you plunge deepest into the mystery of the incarnate God, you can never reach the bottom of it. "No man knoweth the Son, but the Father" (Matt. 11:27). And yet you do know His name, for you know that He is the Word of God. And what does that mean? Why, when a man would show himself, he speaks. "Speak," said the philosopher, "that I may see you." A man's speech is the embodiment of his thought. You know his thought when you hear his word if he is a truth-speaking man. Christ is God's Word. That is His heart, spoken to you. His inmost thoughts of love are printed in great capital letters and set before you in the living, loving, bleeding, dying person of the incarnate Son of God. Thus is He called the Word of God, and in that capacity it is our opportunity to delight ourselves exceedingly in Him and to rejoice because He is now riding triumphantly upon His white horse.

His Followers

"And the armies which were in heaven followed him upon white horses." See, then, that *Christ has a great following*—not one army, but "armies," whole hosts of them—numbers that cannot be counted. My Lord is not the chief of a small band, but He has a great host. There are some who think that all Christ's followers go to their little Bethel and sit down on the top of their own Mount Zion and sweetly bless the Lord, who shuts out the rest of mankind. But I tell you, your little Bethel would not make a stable for the horses of His lieutenants. He has great armies following Him, for a countless number out of every people and nation and tongue has He redeemed with His most precious blood.

And these who follow Him are *all mounted*. They follow Him on white horses. They are mounted on the same sort of horse as Himself, for they fare as He fares: when He walks, they must walk; when He bears a cross, they must carry crosses, too; but if ever He gets a crown, He cries, "They shall be crowned, too." If ever He gets on horseback, He will have His saints on horseback with Him, for it is not like Him that He should ride and they should walk. Remember how Alexander the Great kept up the spirit of his soldiers? Whenever the troops were thirsty, Alexander would not drink, and when they marched on foot, Alexander footed it with them. So it is with our Master. He has been marching here in the rough ways with us, and He will let us ride in the glory ways with Him when the time shall come.

The armies of Christ followed Him on white horses. Look closely at these white horses, for I want you to observe the armor of their riders. Cromwell's men wore at their side long iron scabbards that carried their swords, which oftentimes they wiped across the manes of their horses when they were red with blood. But if you look at these troops, there is not a sword among them. No scabbard dangles, no piece of metal flashes back the sunlight. Neither helmet nor armor is there. They are not armed with lance or pike, and yet they are riding forth to war. Do you want to know the armor of that war? I will tell you. They are clothed in white linen, white and clean. Strange battle array is this! And yet this is how they conquer and how you must conquer, too. This is both armor and weapon. If we but live as Christ lives and follow Him, we shall conquer, for no sword can come at him who lives to God— since, should it slay his body, it cannot touch his soul: he lives and conquers still. Think of this and never ask for any other covering but this in the day of battle.

Yet I have said that they were all on horses, which shows you that the saints of God have a strength that they sometimes forget. You may not realize that you ride on a horse, O child of God, but there is a supreme invisible power that helps you in contending for Christ and for His truth. You are mightier than you know, and you are riding more swiftly to the battle and more rapidly over the heads of your foes than ever you dream. When a door shall be opened in heaven to you and you get to the battle's end, you will say, "Bless the Lord, I, too, rode on a white horse. I, too, conquered when I thought I was defeated. I, too, by simple obedience to His will and keeping the faith and walking in His truth, have been more than a conqueror through Him who loved me."

Is this not a grand sight, this man—this bonny man, as Rutherford calls Him—on His white horse, and all these bright ones following after Him in all their glorious array!

The Warfare

What is the warfare? There cannot be war without a sword, yet if you look all along the ranks of the white-robed armies, there is no sword among them. Who carries the sword? There is one who bears it for them all. It is He, the King, who comes to marshal us. He bears a sword. But where? It is in His mouth! Strange place! A sword in His mouth! Yet this is the only sword my Lord and Master wields. Others have conquered with a metal sword, but Christ subdues men with the gospel. We have but to declare the glad tidings of the love of God, for this is the sword of Christ with which He smites the nations. Be His mouth. Tell it to your children in the Sunday-school class, tell the poor on the street corners, tell by your printed pamphlets, if you cannot by your voice, all the story of how He loved us and gave Himself for us, for this is the sword of our warfare; it goes forth from the mouth of Christ. Let us be content to fight with this and nothing else.

But for those who will not yield to it, our Leader has a hand as well as a tongue, and He says that He will rule the nations with a rod of iron; and if you will read history, you will find that all nations that reject the gospel have to suffer for it. I select one instance. The gospel came to Spain centuries ago, and multitudes of the nobility were converted. But then came the accursed

Inquisition that stamped out the gospel in Spain, and to this day the nation cannot rise. It will, I trust, by God's forgiving mercy; but for centuries, she who ruled the nations and covered the deeps with her armadas has been sitting in her poverty and sloth, for Christ has ruled her with a rod of iron, and so will He rule all nations that reject the testimony of His mouth.

If the sword of His mouth is not heeded, then comes the last of this dread warfare—and may God grant that we may never know it—when His foot shall do it, for He treads the winepress of the fierceness and wrath of Almighty God. What a crush must that be that will come upon the clusters of Gomorrah from the foot that once was nailed to the tree! Who stamped that sinner's soul and crushed it down? Was He an angry angel with a sword of fire? It was the Christ of God, the man of love, rejected and despised. Fiercer than a lion on his prey is love when once provoked. When love turns to jealousy, its fires are like coals of juniper that have a violent flame. Beware lest you continue to despise. Submit to the sword of His mouth lest you be smitten by His hand. Be wise when once His hand begins to smite you lest you have to feel His foot, for it is all over then.

May you and I each have a white horse with which to follow Christ. But we never shall unless we are His followers here. We must put on the snow-white garments now. The righteousness of Christ will be given to anyone who accepts Him and believes on Him. And when your snow-white garments are once on, He will give you the horse of His sacred strength, and you, even you, following in the track of your gallant leaders, shall ride on shouting, "Victory, victory, victory, through the blood of the Lamb."

When Christ died, He suffered the penalty of death on the behalf of all His people, and therefore no believer now dies by way of punishment for sin, since we cannot dream that a righteous God would exact the penalty twice for one offense. Death since Jesus died is not a penal infliction upon the children of God: as such He has abolished it, and it can never be enforced. So why should the saints die then? A divine change must take place upon the body before it will be prepared for incorruption and glory; and death and the grave are, as it were, the refining pot and the furnace by means of which the body is made ready for its future bliss. Death, it is true that you are not yet destroyed, but our living Redeemer has so changed you that you are no longer death but something other than that name! Saints do not truly die, but they are dissolved and depart. Death is the loosing of the cable that the ship may freely sail to the fair havens. Death is the fiery chariot in which we ascend to God; it is the gentle voice of the Great King, who comes into His banqueting hall and says, "Friend, come up higher." Behold, on eagle's wings we mount, we fly, far from this land of mist and cloud, into eternal serenity and brilliance of God's own house above. Yes, our Lord has abolished death. The sting of death is sin, and our great Substitute has taken that sting away by His great sacrifice. Stingless, death abides among the people of God, but it so little harms them that to them it is not death to die.

Chapter Four

Christ the Destroyer of Death

The last enemy that shall be destroyed is death
                                —1 Corinthians 15:26.

HOW WONDERFULLY IS OUR LORD Jesus *one with man!* When the psalmist David had considered the "heavens, the work of [God's] fingers," he said to the Lord, "What is man, that thou art mindful of him? and the son of man, that thou visitest him?" (Ps. 8:3–4). David was speaking of Christ. You would have thought he was thinking of man in his humblest estate and that he was wondering that God should be pleased to honor so frail a being as the poor fallen son of Adam. You would never have dreamed that the glorious gospel lay hid within those words of grateful adoration. Yet in the course of that meditation David went on to say, "Thou madest him to have dominion over the works of thy hands; thou hast put all things under his feet" (vs. 6).

Had it not been for the interpretation of the Holy Spirit, we would still have considered that David was speaking of men in general and of man's natural dominion over the animal creation. But behold, while that is true, there is another and a far more important truth concealed within it, for David, as a prophet, was all the while chiefly speaking of the man of men, the model man, the second Adam, the head of the new race of men. It was of Jesus, the Son of man, as honored of the Father, that the psalmist sang, "thou hast put all things under his feet." Strange, is it not, that when he spoke of man, he must of necessity have spoken also of our Lord? And yet, when we consider the matter, it is only natural and according to truth and remarkable to us only because in our minds we too often consider Jesus and man as far removed and too little regard Him as truly one with man.

Now, see how the apostle Paul infers from the psalm the necessity of the resurrection, for if all things must be put under the feet of the man Christ Jesus, then every form of evil must be conquered by Him, and death among the rest. "For he must reign, till he hath put all enemies under his feet" (1 Cor. 15:25). It must be so, and therefore death itself must ultimately be overcome. Thus out of that simple sentence in the psalm, which we would have understood far different without the light of the Holy Spirit, the apostle gathers the doctrine of the resurrection. The Holy Spirit taught His servant Paul how by a subtle chemistry he could distill from simple words a precious fragrant essence that the common reader never suspected to be there. Texts have their secret drawers, their box within a box, their hidden souls that lie asleep till He who placed them on their secret couches awakens them that they may speak to the hearts of His chosen.

Could you ever have guessed that the resurrection was a part of Psalm 8? No, nor could you have believed, had it not been told to you, that there is fire in the flint, oil in the rock, and bread in the earth we tread upon. Man's books have usually far less in them than we expect, but the Book of the Lord is full of surprises; it is a mass of light, a mountain of priceless revelations. We little know what lies hidden within the Scriptures. We know the form of sound words as the Lord has taught it to us, and by it we find life, but there are inner storehouses into which we have not peered, chambers of revelation lit up with bright lamps, perhaps too bright for our eyes at the present. If Paul, when the Spirit of God rested upon him, could see so much in the songs of David, the day may come when we also shall see still more in the epistles of Paul and wonder at ourselves that we did not understand better the things that the Holy Spirit has so freely spoken to us by the apostles. May we be enabled to look deep and far and behold the sublime glories of our risen Lord.

Death an Enemy

Death was born an enemy, even as Haman the Agagite was the enemy of Israel by his descent (Esth. 8:3). Death is the child of our direst foe, for "sin, when it is finished, bringeth forth death" (James 1:15). Note that that which is distinctly the fruit of transgression cannot be other than an enemy of man. Death was introduced into the world on that gloomy day that saw our fall, and he who had the power of it is our archenemy and betrayer, the devil: from both of which facts we must regard it as the manifest enemy of man. Death is an alien in this world; it did not enter into the original design of the unfallen creation, but its intrusion mars and spoils the whole. Death has no part of the Great Shepherd's flock, but it is a wolf that comes to kill and to destroy. Man in his folly welcomed Satan and sin when they forced their way into the high festival of Paradise, but he never welcomed death; even his blind eyes could see in that skeleton form a cruel foe. As the lion to the herds of the plain, as the scythe to the flowers of the field, as the wind to the dry leaves of the forest, such is death to the sons of men. Men fear death by an inward instinct because their conscience tells them that it is the child of their sin.

Death is well called an enemy, for *it does an enemy's work* toward us. For what purpose does an enemy come but to root up and to pull down and to destroy? Death tears in pieces the wondrous handiwork of God, the fabric of the human body, so marvelously wrought by the fingers of divine skill. The grave is the ruthless destroyer of this rich embroidery. This building of our manhood is a house that is fair to look upon, but death the destroyer darkens its windows, shakes its pillars, closes its doors, and causes the sound of all activity to cease. Then the daughters of music are brought low, and the strong men bow themselves. This pillager spares no work of life, however full of wisdom or beauty, for it looses the silver cord and breaks the golden bowl. The costly pitcher is utterly broken and dashed in pieces. Death is a fierce invader of the realms of life, and where it comes it takes down every good tree, stops all wells of water, and mars every good piece of land with stones. How the beauty is turned to ashes and corruption. Surely an enemy has done this.

Look at the course of death throughout all ages and in all lands. What field is there without its grave? What city without its cemetery? Departed generations of men sleep beneath the grassy hills all around the world. Even the sea is not without mankind's dead. As if the earth were all too crowded with corpses, some of the bodies of the dead have been cast into the caverns. Our enemy, death, has marched as it were with sword and fire ravaging the human race, leaving none to escape. Everywhere it has withered the joys of homes and created sorrow and sighing; in all lands where the sun is seen it has blinded men's eyes with weeping. The tear of the bereaved, the wail of the widow, the moan of the orphan—these have been death's war music, and he has found therein a song of victory.

The greatest conquerors and the cruelest despots have only been death's slaughtermen, journeymen butchers working in his factory. War is nothing more than death holding carnival and devouring his prey a little more in haste than in his common manner.

Death has done the work of an enemy to those of us who have as yet escaped his arrows. Those who have recently stood around a newly dug grave and buried half their hearts can tell you what an enemy death is. It takes the friend from our side, the child from the bosom, neither does it care for our crying. He has fallen who was the pillar of the home; she has been stolen away who was the brightness of the family. The little one is torn out of its mother's bosom though its loss almost breaks her heartstrings; and the blooming youth is taken from his father's side though the parent's fondest hopes are thereby crushed. Death has no pity for the young and no mercy for the old; he pays no regard to the good or to the beautiful. His scythe cuts down sweet flowers and noxious weeds with equal readiness. He comes into our garden, tramples down our lilies, and scatters our roses on the ground. Even the most modest flowers planted in the corner and hiding their beauty beneath the leaves that they may blush unseen, death spies out even these and cares nothing for their fragrance but withers them with his burning breath. He is your enemy, indeed.

Especially is death an enemy to the living when he invades God's house and causes the prophet and the priest to be numbered with the dead. The church mourns when her most useful ministers are struck down, when the watchful eye is closed in darkness and the instructive tongue is silenced. Yet how often does death thus war against us! The most sincere and godly are taken from us. Those mightiest in prayer, those most affectionate in heart, those most exemplary in life, these are cut down in the midst of their labors, leaving behind them a church that needs them more than tongue can tell. If the Lord does but threaten to permit death to seize a beloved pastor, the souls of his people are full of grief, and they view death as their worst foe while they plead with the Lord and entreat Him to bid their minister live.

Even *those who die* may well count death to be their enemy. I do not mean those who have risen to their seats and, as disembodied spirits, behold the King in His beauty, but before this while death was approaching them. Death seemed to their trembling flesh to be a foe, for it is not in our nature, except in moments of extreme pain or abnormality of mind or excessive expectation of glory, for us to be in love with death. It is wise of our Creator to constitute us so that the soul loves the body and the body loves the soul and they desire to dwell together as long as they may, or else there would have been no care for self-preservation, and suicide would have destroyed the human race. It is a first law of our nature that "skin for skin, yea, all that a man hath will he give for his life" (Job 2:4), and thus we are created to struggle for existence and to avoid that which would destroy us. This useful instinct renders death an enemy, but it also aids in keeping us from that crime of all crimes, if a man commits it willfully and in his sound mind—self-murder.

When death comes even to the good man, he comes as an enemy, for he is accompanied by such terrible and grim heralds as do greatly frighten us. None of the illnesses and other means that death takes our lives by add a particle of beauty. Death comes with pains and griefs, he comes with sighs and tears. Clouds and darkness are round about him, an atmosphere laden with dust oppresses those whom he approaches, and a cold wind chills them even to the depths. He rides on the pale horse, and where his steed sets its foot the land becomes a desert. When we forget other grand truths and remember only these dreadful things, death is the king of terrors to us. Hearts are sickened because of him.

But, indeed, he is an enemy, for what does he come to do to our body? I know that what he does will ultimately lead to my body's betterment, but still it is that which in itself, and for the present, is not joyous but grievous. He comes to take the light from the eyes, the hearing from the ears, the speech from the tongue, the activity from the hand, and the thought from the brain. He comes to transform the living man into a mass of corruption, to degrade the beloved form of a loved one to such a condition that affection itself cries out, "Bury my dead out of my sight" (Gen. 23:4). Death, you child of sin, Christ has transformed you marvelously, but in yourself you are an enemy before whom flesh and blood tremble, for they know that you are the murderer of all mankind whose thirst for human prey the blood of nations cannot satisfy.

If you think for a few moments of this enemy, you will observe some of his points of character. He is the *common* foe of all God's people and the enemy of all men. However some have been persuaded that they should not die, yet there is no discharge in this war. And if in this conscription a man escapes the ballot year after year until his gray beard seems to defy the winter's hardest frost, yet must the man of iron yield at last. It is appointed unto all men once to die (Heb. 9:27). The strongest man has no potion of eternal life by which to renew his youth amid the decay of age, nor has the wealthiest prince a price with which to bribe destruction. To the grave must you descend, O crowned monarch, for scepters and shovels are cousins. To the sepulcher you must go down, O mighty man of valor, for the sword and spade are of the same metal. The prince is brother to the worm and must dwell in the same house. Of our whole race it is true, "dust thou art, and unto dust shalt thou return" (Gen. 3:19).

Death is also a *subtle* foe, lurking everywhere, even in the most harmless things. Who can tell where death has not prepared his ambushes? He meets us both at home and abroad; at the table he assails men in their food, and at the fountain he poisons their drink. He strikes in the streets as well as in our beds; he rides on the storm of the sea and walks with us when we are on our way upon the solid land. Where can we fly to escape from you, O death, for from the summit of the Alps men have fallen to their graves, and in the deep places of the earth where the miner goes down to find the precious ore, there you have sacrificed many victims. Death is a subtle foe, and with noiseless footfalls he follows close to our heels when we least think of him.

Death is an enemy whom *none of us will be able to avoid*, take what paths we may, nor can we escape from him when our hour comes. Into this fowler's net, like a bird, we shall fly; in his great seine must all the fish of the great sea of life be taken when their day is come. As surely as the sun sets or as the midnight stars at length descend beneath the horizon or as the waves sink back into the sea, so must we all early or late come to our end and disappear from earth to be known no more among the living.

Sudden, too, are the assaults of this enemy. With a psalm upon the lips a person passes away without a moment's notice. Sudden deaths are as common as slow deaths. Thus is death a foe not to be despised or trifled with. Let us remember all his characteristics, and we shall not be inclined to think lightly of the grim enemy whom our glorious Redeemer has destroyed.

An Enemy to Be Destroyed

Remember that our Lord Jesus Christ has already wrought a great victory upon death so that He has delivered us from lifelong bondage through its fear. He has not yet *destroyed death*, but He has gone very near to it, for we are told that He has "abolished death, and hath brought life and immortality to light through the gospel" (2 Tim. 1:10). This surely must come very near to having destroyed death altogether.

In the first place, our Lord has subdued death in the very worst sense by having delivered His people from spiritual death. "And you hath he quickened, who were dead in trespasses and sins" (Eph. 2:1). Once you had no divine life whatever, but the death of original depravity remained upon you, and so you were dead to all divine and spiritual things. But now, the Spirit of God, even He who raised up Jesus Christ from the dead, has raised you up into newness of life, and you have become new creatures in Christ Jesus. In this sense death has been subdued.

Our Lord in His lifetime also conquered death by restoring certain individuals to life. There were three memorable cases in which at His word the last enemy gave up his prey. Our Lord went into the ruler's house and saw the little girl who had fallen asleep in death and around whom they wept and lamented. He heard their scornful laughter when He said, "She is not dead, but sleepeth," and He put them all out and said to her, "Maid, arise" (Luke 8:52, 54). Then was the spoiler spoiled and the dungeon door set open. Jesus stopped the funeral procession at the gates of Nain when they were carrying out a young man, "the only son of his mother...a widow," and He said, "Young man, I say unto thee, Arise" (Luke 7:12, 14). When the young man sat up and our Lord delivered him to his mother, then again was the prey taken from the mighty. Chief of all, when Lazarus had lain in the grave so long that his sister said, "Lord, by this time he stinketh" (John 11:39), and when, in obedience to the word "Lazarus, come forth" (vs. 43), came forth the raised with his graveclothes still around him but yet really alive, then was death seen to be subservient to the Son of man. "Loose him, and let him go," said the conquering Christ (vs. 44), and death's bonds were removed, for the lawful captive was delivered. When at the Redeemer's resurrection many of the saints arose and came out of their graves into the holy city (Matt. 27:52–53), then was the crucified Lord proclaimed to be victorious over death and the grave.

Still, these were but preliminary skirmishes and mere foreshadowings of the grand victory by which death was overthrown. The real triumph was achieved on the cross.

> *He hell in hell laid low;*
> *Made sin, he sin o'erthrew:*
> *Bowed to the grave, destroy'd it so,*
> *And death, by dying, slew.*

When Christ died, He suffered the penalty of death on the behalf of all His people, and therefore no believer now dies by way of punishment for sin, since we cannot dream that a righteous God would exact the penalty twice for one offense. Death since Jesus died is not a penal infliction upon the children of God: as such He has abolished it, and it can never be enforced. So why should the saints die then? A divine change must take place upon the body before it will be prepared for incorruption and glory; and death and the grave are, as it were, the refining pot and the furnace by means of which the body is made ready for its future bliss. Death, it is true that you are not yet destroyed, but our living Redeemer has so changed you that you are no longer death but something other than that name! Saints do not truly die, but they are dissolved and depart. Death is the loosing of the cable that the ship may freely sail to the fair havens. Death is the fiery chariot in which we ascend to God; it is the gentle voice of the Great King, who comes into His banqueting hall and says, "Friend, come up higher." Behold, on eagle's wings we mount, we fly, far from this land of mist and cloud, into eternal serenity and brilliance of God's own house above. Yes, our Lord has abolished death. The sting of death is sin, and our great Substitute has taken that sting away by His great sacrifice. Stingless, death abides among the people of God, but it so little harms them that to them it is not death to die.

Further, Christ vanquished death and thoroughly overcame him when He rose. What a temptation one has to paint a picture of the resurrection, but I will not be led aside to attempt more than a few strokes. When our Champion awoke from His brief sleep of death and found Himself in the cavern of the grave, He quietly proceeded to put off the garments of the tomb. How leisurely He proceeded! He folded up the napkin and placed it by itself, that those who lose their friends might wipe their eyes with it; and then He took off the winding sheet and laid the graveclothes by themselves that they might be there when His saints came there, so that the chamber might be well furnished and the bed ready sheeted and prepared for their rest. The sepulcher is no longer an empty vault, a dreary chamber of rest, a dormitory furnished and prepared, hung with the tapestry that Christ Himself has bequeathed. It is now no more a damp, dark, dreary prison; Jesus has changed all that.

The angel from heaven rolled away the stone from our Lord's sepulcher and let in the fresh air and light again upon our Lord, who stepped out more than a conqueror. Death had fled. The grave had capitulated.

> *Lives again our glorious King!*
> *Where, O death, is now thy sting?*
> *Once He died our souls to save;*
> *Where's thy victory, boasting grave?*

As surely as Christ rose, so did He guarantee as an absolute certainty the resurrection of all His saints into a glorious life for their bodies, the life of their souls never having paused even for a moment. In this He conquered death, and since that memorable victory, every day Christ is overcoming death, for He gives His Spirit to His saints. And having that Spirit within them, they meet the last enemy without alarm. Often they confront him with songs; perhaps more frequently they face him with calm countenance and fall asleep with peace. I will not fear you, death, why should I? You look like a dragon, but your sting is gone. Your teeth are broken, old lion, so why should I fear you? I know you are no more able to destroy me, but you are sent as a messenger to conduct me to the golden gates where I shall enter and see my Savior's unveiled face forever.

To die has been so different a thing from what many expected it to be, so joyous and light. Many have been so unloaded of all care, have felt so relieved instead of burdened, that they have wondered whether this could be the monster they had been so afraid of all their days. They find it a pin's prick, whereas they feared it would prove a sword thrust. It is the shutting of the eye on earth and the opening of it in heaven, whereas they thought it would have been a stretching upon the rack or a dreary passage through a dismal region of gloom and dread. Beloved, our exalted Lord has overcome death in all these ways.

But now, observe, that this is not the text—the text speaks of something yet to be done. The last enemy that *shall be* destroyed is death, so that death in the sense meant by the text is not destroyed yet. He is to be destroyed, and how will that be? I take it that death will be destroyed in the sense, first, that at the coming of Christ, *those who are alive and remain shall not see death*. They shall be changed; there must be a change even to the living before they can inherit eternal life, but they shall not actually die. The multitude of the Lord's own who will be alive at His coming will pass into the glory without needing to die. Thus death, as far as they are concerned, will be destroyed.

But the sleeping ones, the myriads who have left their flesh and bones in the grave, death shall be destroyed even as to them, for when the trumpet sounds, they shall rise from the tomb. *The resurrection is the destruction of death.* We never taught or believed that every particle of every body that was put into the grave would come to its other particles and that the absolutely identical material would rise, but we do say that the identical body will be raised and that as surely as there comes out of the ground the seed that was put into it, though in very different form as a flower, so surely shall the same body rise again. The same material is not necessary, but there shall come out of the grave, or out of the earth if it never saw a grave, or out of the sea if devoured by monsters, that same body for true identity that was inhabited by the soul while here below. Was it not so with our Lord? Even so shall it be with His own people, and then shall be brought to pass the saying that is written, "Death is swallowed up in victory. O death, where is thy sting? O grave, where is thy victory?" (1 Cor. 15:54–55).

There will be this feature in our Lord's victory, that death will be fully destroyed because *those who rise will not be one bit the worse off for having died*. I believe concerning those new bodies that there will be no trace upon them of the feebleness of old age, none of the marks of long and wearying sickness, none of the scars of martyrdom. Death shall not have left his mark upon them at all, except it is some glory mark that shall be to their honor, like the scars in the flesh of the Son of God, which are His chief beauty even now in the eyes of those for whom His hands and feet were pierced. In this sense, death shall be destroyed because he shall have done no damage to the saints at all, the very trace of decay shall have been swept away from the redeemed.

And then, finally, there shall, after this trumpet of the Lord, be *no more death* or sorrow or crying or pain, for the former things shall have passed away (Rev. 21:4). "Christ being raised from the dead dieth no more; death hath no more dominion over him" (Rom. 6:9). And so also the ones whom He has made alive, His own redeemed, they too shall die no more. What a dreadful supposition that they should ever have to undergo temptation or pain or death a second time! It cannot be! Because Christ lives, we live also.

Death Is to Be Destroyed Last

Because death came in last, he must go out last. Death was not the first of our foes: first came the devil, then sin, then death. Death is not the worst of enemies; death is an enemy, but he is much to be preferred to our other adversaries. It were better to die a thousand times than to sin. To be tried by death is nothing compared with being tempted by the devil. The mere physical pains connected with death are comparative trifles compared with the hideous grief that is caused by sin and the burden that a sense of guilt causes to the soul. No, death is but a secondary mischief compared with the defilement of sin. Let the great enemies go down first; smite the shepherd and the sheep will be scattered; let sin and Satan, the lord of all these evils, be struck first, and death may well be left to the last.

Notice that death is the last enemy to each individual Christian and the last to be destroyed. If the Word of God says it is last, I want to remind you of a little piece of practical wisdom—let him be the last. Do not dispute the appointed order, but let the last be last. I have known believers who wanted grace to vanquish death long before they died. Why would God provide dying grace till the dying moment, and why would we want it? A boat will be needful only when we reach a river. Ask for living grace and glorify Christ by it, and then you shall have dying grace when dying time comes. Your enemy is going to be destroyed, but not today. There is a great host of enemies to be fought today, and you may be content to let this one alone for a while. This enemy will be destroyed, but of the times and the season we are in ignorance; our wisdom is to be good soldiers of Jesus Christ as the duty of every day requires.

Take your trials as they come! As the enemies march up, slay them, rank upon rank, but if you fail in the name of God to smite the front ranks and say, "No, I am only afraid of the rear rank," then you are playing the fool. Leave the final adversary till that enemy advances, and meanwhile hold your place in the conflict. God will in due time help you to overcome your last enemy, but meanwhile see to it that you overcome the world, the flesh, and the devil. If you live well, you shall die well. That same covenant in which the Lord Jesus gave you life contains also the grant of death, for "all things are yours; whether Paul, or Apollos, or Cephas, or the world, or life, or death, or things present, or things to come; all are yours; and ye are Christ's; and Christ is God's" (1 Cor. 3:21–23).

Why is death left to the last? I think it is because Christ can make much use of him. Death serves a great service before he is destroyed. What lessons some of us have learned from death! How often death has served to make us feel that these poor fleeting toys on earth are not worth living for, that as others pass away so must we also be gone, and thus they help to set loose the things of this world and urge us to take wing and mount toward the world to come. There are, perhaps, no sermons like the deaths that have happened in our households; the departure of our friends have been to us solemn teachings of divine wisdom, which our heart could not help hearing. So Christ has spared death to make him a preacher to His saints.

And you know that if there had been no death, the saints of God would not have had the opportunity to exhibit the highest ardor of their love. Where has love for Christ triumphed most? Why, in the death of the martyrs. O Christ, You never had such garlands woven for You by human hands as they have brought You who have come up to heaven from the forests of persecution, having waded through streams of blood. By death for Christ, the saints have glorified Him most. So is it in their measure with saints who die from ordinary deaths; they would have had no such test for faith and work for patience as they now have if there had been no death. Part of the reason for the continuance of this dispensation is that the Christ of God may be glorified, but if believers never died, the supreme consummation of faith's victory must have been unknown.

If I may die as I have seen some of my church members die, I court the grand occasion. I would not wish to escape death by some byroad if I may sing as they sang. If I may have such hosannas and hallelujahs beaming in my very eyes as I have seen as well as heard from them, it were a blessed thing to die. Yes, as a supreme test of love and faith, death is well postponed awhile to let the saints glorify their Master.

Besides, without death we should not be so conformed to Christ as we shall be if we fall asleep in Him. If there could be any jealousies in heaven among the saints, I think that any saint who does not die but is changed when Christ comes could almost meet me and you, who have died, and say, "Brother, there is one thing I have missed. I never lay in the grave, I never had the chill hand of death laid on me, and so in that I was not conformed to my Lord. But *you* know what it is to have fellowship with Him, even in His death."

Death is not yet destroyed, because he brings the saints home. He does but come to them and whisper his message, and in a moment they are supremely blessed. And so death is not destroyed yet, for he answers useful purposes. But he is going to be destroyed. He is the last enemy of the Church collectively. The Church as a body has had a mass of foes to contend with, but after the resurrection, we shall say, "There are no other foes left."

Eternity shall roll on in ceaseless bliss. There may be changes, bringing new delights. Perhaps in the eternity to come there may be eras and ages of yet more amazing bliss and still more superlative ecstasy. But there shall be "no rude alarm of raging foes, no cares to break the last repose."

The last enemy that shall be destroyed is death, and if the last be slain, there can be no future foe. The battle is fought, and the victory is won forever. And who has won it but the Lamb who sits upon the throne, to whom let us ascribe honor and glory and majesty and power and dominion and might, forever and ever. Amen.

Another thought that is full of comfort springs up in my mind. Remember the crowns of Christ's head and be comforted. Is providence against you? If you think so, you are in error. God has not become your enemy. Providence is not against you, because Jesus is its King; He weights its trials and counts its storms. Your enemies may strive, but they shall not prevail against you—He will smite them upon the cheekbone. Are you passing through the fire? The fire is Christ's dominion. Are you going through the floods? They shall not drown you, for even the floods obey the voice of the omnipotent Messiah. Wherever you are called, you cannot go where Jesus' love does not reign. Commit yourself into His hands. However dark your circumstances, He can make your pathway clear. Though night surround you, He shall surely bring the day. Only trust greatly in His Almighty hands, and you shall yet see how kind His heart, how strong His hand to bring you out. Come bring your burdens to His feet and take a song away. If your heart is heavy, bring them to Him; the golden scepter can lighten them. If your griefs are many, tell them into His ear; His loving eyes can scatter them, and through the thick darkness there shall be a bright light shining, and you shall see His face and know that all is well.

Chapter Five

The Savior's Many Crowns

And on his head were many crowns—Revelation 19:12.

WE KNOW THIS HEAD WELL and have not forgotten its marvelous history. A head that in infancy reclined on the bosom of a woman! A head that was meekly bowed in obedience to a carpenter! A head that became in later years a reservoir of tears. A head whose "sweat was as it were great drops of blood falling down to the ground" (Luke 22:44). A head that was spit upon, whose hair was plucked! A head that at the last in the grim agony of death, crowned with thorns, gave utterance to the terrible death cry—*lama sabachthani*! A head that afterward slept in the grave, and—glory be to Him who lives and was dead but is alive forevermore—a head that afterward rose again from the tomb and looked with radiant eyes of love upon the holy women waiting at the sepulcher. This is the head of which John speaks in the words of the text. Who would have thought that a head, the visage of which was more marred than that of any other man, a head that suffered more from the tempests of heaven and of earth than ever mortal brow before, should now be surrounded with these many diadems, these star-bestudded crowns!

It requires John himself to expound this glorious vision. Alas, my eye has not yet seen the heavenly glory, nor has my ear heard the celestial song! I am therefore but as a little child among topless mountains, overawed with grandeur and speechless with wonder. With the divine aid of the Spirit of God, I will attempt to look upon the glorious diadems of our Lord and King. The crowns upon the head of Christ are of three kinds. First, there are the *crowns of dominions*, many of which are on His head. Next, there are the *crowns of victory* that He has won in many a terrible battle. Then there are the *crowns of thanksgiving* with which His Church and all His people have delighted to crown His wondrous head.

Crowns of Dominion

Let every believing eye look through the thick darkness and behold Jesus as He sits this day upon the throne of His Father, and let every heart rejoice while it sees the many crowns of dominion upon His head. First and foremost, there sparkles about His brow the everlasting diadem of the King of *heaven*. His are the angels. The cherubim and seraphim continually sound forth His praise. At His command the mightiest spirit delights to fly and carry His orders to the most distant worlds. He has but to speak and it is done. Cheerfully is He obeyed, and majestically does He reign. His high courts are thronged with holy spirits, who live upon His smile, who drink light from His eyes, who borrow glory from His majesty.

There is no spirit in heaven so pure that it does not bow before Him, no angel so bright that it does not veil its face with its wings when it draws near to Him. Moreover, the many spirits redeemed delight to bow before Him. Day without night they circle His throne, singing, "Worthy is the Lamb that was slain to receive power, and riches, and wisdom, and strength, and honour, and glory, and blessing" (Rev. 5:12). To be King of heaven is surely enough! Christ is Lord of all creation. He laid the precious stones upon which was built that city that has foundations, whose builder and maker is God. God is the light of that city and the joy of its inhabitants, whose loving life it is evermore to pay Him honor.

Side by side with this bright crown of heaven behold another. It is the iron crown of *hell*, for Christ reigns there supreme. Not only in the dazzling brightness of heaven but also in the black impenetrable darkness of hell is His omnipotence felt and His sovereignty acknowledged. The chains that bind damned spirits are the chains of His strength; the fires that burn are the fires of His vengeance; the burning rays that scorch through their eyeballs and melt their very heart are flashed from His vindictive eye. There is no power in hell besides His. The very devils know His might. He chains the great dragon. If He gives him a temporary liberty, yet is the chain in His hand, and He can draw the dragon back lest he go beyond his limit. Hell trembles before Him. The very howlings of lost spirits are but deep bass notes of His praise. While in heaven the glorious notes shout forth His goodness, in hell the deep growlings resound His justice and His certain victory over all His foes. Thus His empire is higher than the highest heaven and deeper than the lowest hell.

This earth also is a province of His wide domains. Though the empire is small compared with others, from this world, He has perhaps derived more glory than from any other part of His dominions. He reigns on earth. On His head is the crown of *creation*. "All things were made by him; and without him was not any thing made that was made" (John 1:3). His voice said, "Let there be light" (Gen. 1:3), and there was light. It was His strength that piled the mountains, and His wisdom balanced the clouds. He is Creator. If you lift your eyes to the upper spheres and behold the farthest starry world, He made them. They are not self-created. He struck them off like sparks from the anvil of His omnipotence; and there they glitter, upheld and supported by His might. He made the earth and all men that are upon it. The sea is His, and He made it also. Leviathan He has formed, and though that monster makes the deep to be hoary, yet it is but a creature of His power.

Together with this crown of creation there is another—the crown of *providence*, for He sustains all things by the word of His power. Everything must cease to be if it were not for the continual outgoing of His strength. The earth must die, the sun must grow dim, and nature sink in years if Christ did not supply it with perpetual strength. He sends the howling blasts of winter; He, anon, restrains them and breathes the breath of spring; He ripens the fruits of summer; and He makes glad the autumn of His harvest. All things know His will. The heart of the great universe beats by His power; the very sea derives its tide from Him. Let Him once withdraw His hands, and the pillars of earth must tremble, the stars must fall like fig leaves, and all things must be quenched in the blackness of annihilation. On His head is the crown of providence.

And next to providence there glitters also the thrice-glorious crown of grace. He is the King of *grace*: He gives, or He withholds. The river of God's mercy flows from underneath His throne; He sits as Sovereign in the dispensation of mercy. He has the key of heaven; He opens, and no man shuts; He shuts, and no man opens; He called, and the stubborn heart obeys; He wills, and the rebellious spirit bends his knee, for He is Master of men, and when He wills to bless, none can refuse the benediction. He reigns in His Church amid willing spirits; and He reigns for His Church over all the nations of the world, that He may gather unto Himself a people that no man can number who bow before the scepter of His love.

I pause here, overcome by the majesty of the subject, and instead of attempting to describe that head and those glittering crowns, I shall act the part of a seraph and bow before that well-crowned head and cry, "Holy, holy, holy, are You Lord God of hosts! The keys of heaven and death and hell hang at Your side. You are supreme, and unto You be glory forever and ever."

How do you respond to this? Do these thoughts not stir your heart? I think I hear one say, "If this is so, if Christ has these many crowns of dominion, how vain it is for me to rebel against Him." Perhaps like Saul of Tarsus you have become "exceedingly mad" against Him (Acts 26:11). You hate the very name of Christ, you curse His servants, you despise His Word. You would, if you could, persecute His followers. This you should know, that you have undertaken a battle in which you are certain of defeat. Whoever strove against God and prospered? Go and do battle against the lightning and hold the thunderbolt in your hand; go and restrain the sea and hush the tempest in the hollow of your hand; and when you have done this, then lift your puny hand against the King of kings. For He who was crucified is your Master, and though you oppose Him, you shall not succeed. In your utmost malice you shall be defeated, and the vehemence of your wrath shall but return upon your own head.

I think I see this day the multitudes of Christ's enemies. They stand up and take counsel together, saying, "Let us break their bands asunder, and cast away their cords from us" (Ps. 2:3). Can you hear the distant deep-sounding laugh? Out of the thick darkness of His tabernacle, Jehovah laughs and declares, "Yet have I set my king upon my holy hill of Zion" (vs. 6). Come on in your most mighty force and fall like the waves that are broken against the immovable rock. He rules and He will rule, and you one day shall be made to feel His power. So that "at the name of Jesus every knee should bow, of things in heaven, and things in earth, and things under the earth" (Phil. 2:10).

Another thought that is full of comfort springs up in my mind. Remember the crowns of Christ's head and be comforted. Is providence against you? If you think so, you are in error. God has not become your enemy. Providence is not against you, because Jesus is its King; He weights its trials and counts its storms. Your enemies may strive, but they shall not prevail against you—He will smite them upon the cheekbone. Are you passing through the fire? The fire is Christ's dominion. Are you going through the floods? They shall not drown you, for even the floods obey the voice of the omnipotent Messiah. Wherever you are called, you cannot go where Jesus' love does not reign. Commit yourself into His hands. However dark your circumstances, He can make your pathway clear. Though night surround you, He shall surely bring the day. Only trust greatly in His Almighty hands, and you shall yet see how kind His heart, how strong His hand to bring you out. Come bring your burdens to His feet and take a song away. If your heart is heavy, bring them to Him; the golden scepter can lighten them. If your griefs are many, tell them into His ear; His loving eyes can scatter them, and through the thick darkness there shall be a bright light shining, and you shall see His face and know that all is well.

I am sure there is no more delightful doctrine to the believer than that of Christ's absolute sovereignty. I am glad there is no such thing as chance, that nothing is left to itself but that Christ everywhere has sway. If I thought that there was a devil in hell that Christ did not govern, I should be afraid that devil would destroy me. If I thought there was a circumstance on earth that Christ did not overrule, I should fear that that circumstance would ruin me. If there were an angel in heaven that was not one of Jehovah's subjects, I should tremble at him. But since Christ is King of kings and I am one whom He loves, I give all my cares to Him, for He cares for me.

Crowns of Victory

The first diadems that I have mentioned are His by right. He is God's only-begotten and well-beloved Son, and hence He inherits unlimited dominions. But viewed as the Son of Man, conquest has made Him great, and His own right hand and His holy arm have won Him the triumph. In the first place, Christ has a crown that I pray that you may wear. He has a crown of victory over the world. For He has said, "Be of good cheer; I have overcome the world" (John 16:33). Did you ever think of what a stern battle that Christ had to fight with the world? The world first said, "I will extinguish Him, He shall not be known," and it threw on Christ heaps of poverty that there He might be smothered. But God shone in His poverty, and the seamless coat shone with greater light than the robe of the rabbi. Then the world attacked Him with its threatenings. Sometimes they dragged Him to the edge of a hill to cast Him down; at another time they took up stones to stone Him. But He who was not to be hidden by poverty was not to be quenched by threatening. And the world tried its banishments; it came with a fair face and presented to Him a crown. They would have taken Christ and made Him a king, but He who cared not for their frowns was not taken by their smiles. He put away the crown from Him; He came not to be king but to suffer and die.

Have you never thought how through thirty years the world tempted Christ? That temptation of the devil in the wilderness was not the only one that He endured. Trials of every shape and size surrounded Him. The world emptied its quiver and shot all its arrows against the breast of the spotless Redeemer, but all holy, all unharmed was He. Still separate from sinners, He walked among them without defilement, feasted among them and yet did not sanction their gluttony, drank with them and yet was not a drunkard, acted as they acted in all innocent things, and was the world's man and yet not a man of the world. He was in the world, but He was not of it.

I would that we could imitate Christ in our battle with the world. But the world oftentimes gets the upper hand. Sometimes we yield to its smiles, and often we tremble before its frowns. Have hope and courage, believer; be like your Master, be the world's foe and overcome it, yield not, never allow it to entrap your watchful feet. Stand upright amid all its pressure and never be moved by all its enchantments. Christ did this, and therefore around His head is that royal crown of victory, a trophy of triumph over the entire forces of the world.

Furthermore, the next crown He wears is the crown by which He has overcome sin. Sin has been more than a match for creatures of every kind. Sin fought the angels, and a third part of the stars of heaven fell. Sin defied the perfect Adam and soon overcame him, for even at the first blow he fell. Sin had a stern contest with Jesus our Lord, but in Him it found its master. Sin came with all its temptations, but Christ resisted and overcame. It came with its horror and with its curse; Christ suffered, Christ endured, and so He destroyed sin's power. He took the poisoned darts of the curse into His own heart and there quenched its poison fires by shedding His own blood. By suffering, Christ has become master over sin. The dragon's neck is now beneath His feet. There is not a temptation that He has not known and therefore not a sin that He has not overcome. He has cast down every shape and form of evil, and now forever stands He more than a conqueror through His glorious sufferings. How bright that crown that He deserves, who has forever put away our sin by the sacrifice of Himself! My soul enraptured restrains my voice, and once again I bow in spirit before His throne and worship my bleeding Ransomer, my suffering Savior.

Christ also wears about His head the crown of death. He died, and in that dreadful hour He overcame death, rifled the sepulcher, split the stone that guarded the mouth of the grave, hewed death to pieces, and destroyed the archenemy. Christ seized the iron limbs of death and ground them to powder in His hand. Death swayed his scepter over all the bodies of men, but Christ has opened the gate of resurrection for His redeemed. In that day when He shall put the trumpet to His lips and blow the resurrection blast, then shall it be seen how Christ is universal monarch over all the domains of death, for as the Lord our Savior rose, so all His followers must.

Then again, Christ is not only Lord of the world, King of sin and King of death but also King of Satan. He met that archfiend foot to foot. Fearful was the struggle, for our Champion sweat as it were great drops of blood falling to the ground. But He hewed His way to victory through His own body, through the agonies of His own soul. Head and hands and feet and heart were wounded, but the Savior flinched not in the fight. He rent the lion of the pit as though he were a kid and broke the dragon's head in pieces. Satan was nibbling at Christ's heel, but Christ trod on him and smashed his head. Now has Jesus led captivity captive and is master over all the hosts of hell. Glorious is that victory! Angels repeat the triumphant strain, His redeemed take up the song, and you praise Him, too, for He has overcome all the evil of hell itself.

And yet, once again, another crown has Christ, and that is the crown of victory over man. What hard work it is to fight with the evil heart of man. If you wish a man to do evil, you can soon overcome him, but if you would overcome him with good, how hard the struggle! Christ would have man's heart, but man would not give it. Christ tried him in many ways; He wooed him, but man's heart was hard and would not melt. He brought Moses and the law, but that did not change man's heart. He used the fire, the whirlwind, and the hammer of God, but the heart would not break and open to Christ.

Then Christ came with His cross and said, "See, Hardheart, I love you. Though you do not love Me, yet I love you, and in proof of this, see: I will hang on this cross." As Hardheart looked on, suddenly, fierce men nailed the Savior to the tree. Jesus' hands were pierced; His soul was rent with agony, and looking down on Hardheart, Jesus said, "Will you not love Me? I love you; I have redeemed you from death; though you have hated me, yet do I die for you." And Hardheart said, "Jesus, I can bear it no longer. I yield to You. Your love has overcome me. I would gladly be your subject forever." Has Christ ever overcome you? Has His love been too much for you? Have you been compelled to give up your sins, wooed by His love divine? Have your eyes been made to run with tears at the thought of His affection for you and of your own ingratitude? Have you ever thought, "I am the worst of sinners. I have despised the Savior's love. His Bible I have left unread. His blood I have trampled under foot, and yet He died for me and loved me with an everlasting love." Surely, this has made you bow your knee as a willing captive to the Lord.

Crowns of Thanksgiving

"On his head are many crowns." In the first place, all the mighty doers of Christ's Church ascribe their crown to Him. What a glorious crown is that which Elijah will wear—the man who went to King Ahab and, when Ahab said, "Hast thou found me, O mine enemy?" (1 Kings 21:20), reproved the king to his very face— the man who took the prophets of Baal and let not one of them escape but hewed them in pieces and made them a sacrifice to God. What a crown will *he* wear who ascended into heaven in a chariot of fire! What a crown belongs to Daniel, saved from the lions' den—Daniel, the sincere prophet of God. What a crown will be that which shall glitter on the head of the weeping Jeremiah and the eloquent Isaiah! What crowns are those that shall adorn the heads of the apostles! What a weighty diadem is that which Paul shall receive for his tireless years of service! And then, how shall the crown of Luther glitter and the crown of Calvin; and what of Whitefield and Wesley, and all those who have so valiantly served God and who by His might have put to flight the armies of the enemy and have maintained the gospel banner erect in troubled times!

Let me point you to a scene. Elijah enters heaven, and where does he go with that crown that is instantly put upon his head? See, he rushes to the throne, and stooping there, he uncrowns himself: "Not unto me, not unto me, but unto Your name be all the glory!" See the prophets as they stream in one by one; without exception, they put their crowns upon the head of Christ. And note the apostles and all the mighty teachers of the Church; they all bow there and cast their crowns at the feet of Him who, by His grace, enabled them to win them.

Not only the mighty doers but the mighty sufferers do this. How brilliant are the ruby crowns of the martyred saints. From the stake, from the fire, from the hangman's noose, they ascended up to God; and among the bright ones they are doubly bright, fairest of the mighty host that surrounds the throne of the Blessed One. What crowns they wear! An angel might blush to think that his dignity was so small compared with that of those riders in chariots of fire. Where are all those crowns? They are on the head of Christ. Not a martyr wears his crown; they place their fiery crowns upon the head of the Savior, and there I see them all glitter. For it was His love that helped them to endure; it was by His love that they overcame.

And then, think of another list of crowns. Those who turn many to righteousness shall shine as the stars forever and ever. There are a few saints whom God has enabled to do much for the Church and much for the world. They spend and are spent. Their bodies know no rest, their souls no ease. Like chariots instinct with life or dragged by unseen but resistless coursers, they fly from duty to duty. What crowns shall theirs be when they come before God, when the souls they have saved shall enter paradise with them. What shouts of acclamation, what honors, what rewards shall then be given to the winner of souls! What will they do with their crowns? Why, they will take them and lay them there where sits the Lamb in the midst of the throne. These will bow and say, "Jesus, we were not saviors, You did it all. The victory belongs not to us but to our Master. All our success is accomplished through Your strength and by the power of Your grace."

But see, another host approaches. I see a company of cherubic spirits flying upward to Christ. Who are they? I know them not. They are not numbered among the martyrs; I do not read their names among the apostles; I do not even distinguish them as having been written among the saints of the living God. Who are they? I ask one of them, "Who are you bright and sparkling spirits?" The leader replies, "We are the glorious myriad of *infants* who compose the family above. We came straight from our mothers and fled straight to heaven, redeemed by the blood of Christ. From every nation of the earth have we come; from the days of the first infant even to the winding up of earth's history, we in flocks have sped here like doves to our windows." They crown the Savior as well.

But yonder I see another company following them. "Who are you?" I ask. The reply is, "Our history on earth is the very opposite of the story of those bright spirits that have gone before. We lived on earth for sixty or seventy or eighty years, until we tottered into our graves from very weakness. When we died, our hair had grown gray and we were old with age. After many years of strife with the world, of trials and troubles, we entered heaven at last." "And you have crowns, I see." "Yes," they say, "but we do not intend to wear them." "Where are you going?" "We are going to His throne, for our crowns have been given to us by grace, for nothing but grace could have helped us to weather the storm so many years." Together the groups come to cry, "Salvation to our God which sitteth upon the throne, and unto the Lamb" (Rev. 7:10).

Then I see following behind them another class. "And who are you?" Their answer is, "We are the chief of sinners, saved by grace." And there they come—Saul of Tarsus, and Manasseh, and Rahab, and many of the same class. "And how have you come here?" They reply, "We have had much forgiven, we were grievous sinners, but the love of Christ reclaimed us, the blood of Christ washed us; and whiter than snow are we, though once we were black as hell. We are going to cast our crowns at His feet and to crown Him Lord of all." Among them I hope it may be my lot to stand. Washed from my sins, redeemed by precious blood, happy shall that moment be when I shall take my crown from my head and put it on the head of Him whom having not seen I love but in whom believing I rejoice with joy unspeakable and full of glory.

"Ah, but," says Little-faith, "I fear I shall never get there, and therefore I shall never crown Him." Yes, but Little-faith, do you know that one of the richest crowns Christ ever wears and one of the brightest that adorns His head is yours? For when you get to heaven, you will say, "Oh, what grace has been shown to me, that though the lowest of the family, I have still been kept—though the least of all the saints, yet hell has not prevailed against me—though weaker than the weakest, yet as my days so has my strength been." Will not your song be loud when, approaching His dear feet, you lay your honors there?

Have you a crown to put on the head of Jesus Christ? Make this a day of crowning the King of kings and Lord of lords.

To those who are imprisoned in their sin, the word if rings a sweet silver bell of hope. No matter who you are or what you are or how many years you may have remained a slave of Satan, "if the Son therefore shall make you free," the glorious Liberator can make you free. "Wherefore he is able also to save them to the uttermost that come unto God by him" (Heb. 7:25). Perhaps that which weighs upon you most heavily is a sense of your past guilt—you have offended God often, willfully, atrociously, with many aggravations. You feel that all that God's Word says against you is deserved and every threatening that His book utters is your just due. Can so foul a sinner be made clean? I know that the leopard cannot lose its spots nor the Ethiopian change his skin by his own efforts. Is there a power divine that can take away the spots and change your nature? Surely, it already has happened. No sin that you have committed need shut you out of heaven. However damnable your iniquities may have been, there is forgiveness with God that He may be feared. You may have gone to the very edge of hell, but the arm of God's grace is long enough to reach you. You may feel that your tongue is padlocked with blasphemy, your hands bound by acts of atrocious violence, your heart fettered with corruption, your feet chained fast to the satanic blocks of unbelief, your whole self locked up in the bondage of corruption, but there is One so mighty to save that He can set even you free. "The blood of Jesus Christ his Son cleanseth us from all sin" (1 John 1:7).

Chapter Six

The Great Liberator

If the Son therefore shall make you free, ye shall be free indeed
—John 8:36.

BLESSED IS THE WORD *free*, and blessed is He who gives Himself to make me free. When a man successfully breaks the yoke off the neck of the oppressed, you do well to give him your joyous acclamations. But Jesus Christ excels them all and deserves the love of all the good and brave. *Political* slavery is an intolerable evil. To live, to think, to act, to speak, at the permission of another! Better have no life at all! To depend for my existence upon a despot's will is death itself. Cowardly spirits may wear the dog collar that their master puts upon them and cringe at his feet for the bones of his table, but men who are worthy of the name would rather feed the vultures on the field of battle.

The burden of civil bondage is too heavy for bold spirits to bear with patience, and therefore they fret and murmur beneath it. This murmuring the tyrant does not love, and therefore he throws the sufferers into his dungeons and bids them wear out their days in captivity. Blessed is he who hurls down the despot, bursts open the door of his dungeons, and gives true men their rights. We have never felt, and therefore we do not know, the bitterness of slavery.

Our emancipators have gone to the world of spirits, passing on to us the heirloom of liberty, for which we should love their names and reverence their God. If they could have lived on till now, how we should honor them!

But men may have political liberty to the very fullest extent and yet be slaves, for there is such a thing as religious bondage. He who cringes before a pastor or minister may as easily be an abject slave. To be afraid of the mutterings of a religious person, to prostrate reason before the throne of superstition, is slavery indeed. To yield obedience to our Lord, to offer prayer to God Most High, is perfect freedom; but to tell my heart out to a mortal, to trust my family secrets and my wife's character to the commands of a man who imposes spiritual authority is worse than the worst form of serfdom. I would sooner serve the most cruel tyrant who ever crushed humanity beneath his iron heel than bow before a false spiritual authority. You may cut through the bonds of despots with a sword, but the sword of the Lord Himself is needed here. Truth must break these fetters, and the Holy Spirit must open these dungeons. You may escape from prison, but superstition hangs round a man and, with its deadly influence, keeps him ever in its dark and gloomy cell. Skepticism that proposes to snap the chains of superstition only replaces a blind belief with an unhallowed confidence and leaves the victim as oppressed as ever. Blessed are our eyes when we have seen the light of gospel liberty.

Yet a man may be delivered from a religious slavery and still be a slave, for he may still be controlled by the devil or his own lusts, which is much the same. Our carnal desires and inclinations are domineering lords enough, as those know who follow their commands. He may be a slave to his own evil heart; he may be grinding at the mill of greed, rotting in the reeking dungeon of sensuality, dragged along by the chains of maddened anger, or born down by the yoke of fashionable custom. He is the free man who is master of himself through the grace of God. He who serves his own passions is the slave of the worst of despots. Talk to me not about the pits in which men have been immersed and forgotten or of heavy chains and torture racks; the slave of sin and Satan, sooner or later, knows greater horrors than these—his doom more terrible because eternal, and his slavery more hopeless because it is one into which he willingly commits himself.

Perhaps some readers claim liberty for themselves and say that they are able to control their passions and have never given way to impure desires. Some may get as far as that in a modified sense and yet not be free. Perhaps you are one who, knowing the right, have struggled for it against the wrong. You have reformed yourself from sins into which you had fallen. You have by diligence brought the flesh somewhat under, in its outward manifestations of sin, and now your life is moral, your conduct is respectable, your reputation is high. Still, for all that, it may be that you are conscious that you are not free. Your old sins haunt you, your former corruptions perplex you, you have not found peace, for you have not obtained forgiveness. You have buried your sins beneath the earth for years, but conscience has given them a resurrection, and the ghosts of your past transgressions haunt you. Perhaps you can hardly sleep at night because of the recollection of the wrath of God that you deserve. You have not yet come to the full liberty of the children of God, as you will if you cast yourself into the hands of Jesus, who frees the captives. "If the Son therefore shall make you free, ye shall be free indeed"—free as the greatest political liberator cannot make you, free as he cannot make you who merely delivers you from superstition, free as reformation cannot make you, free as God alone can make you by His free Spirit.

My *first* point to those who are in bondage to Satan is that *liberty is possible*. The text would not mock us with a dream: it says, *"If the Son therefore shall make you free."* Not all who are slaves shall be set free, but there is the possibility of liberty implied in the text. Blessed "if." It is like the prison window through the stony wall: it lets in enough sunshine for us to read the word *hope* with. *Second, there is a false freedom.* You see that in the text as well—"Ye shall be free *indeed*." There were some who professed to be free but were not so. The Greek is, "Ye shall be free *really*," for there are some who are free only in name and in the shadow of freedom but who are not free as to the substance. *Third, real freedom must come to us from the Son,* the glorious Son of God who, being free and giving Himself to us, gives us freedom.

Freedom Is Possible

To those who are imprisoned in their sin, the word *if* rings a sweet silver bell of hope. No matter who you are or what you are or how many years you may have remained a slave of Satan, *"if* the Son therefore shall make you free," the glorious Liberator can make you free. "Wherefore he is able also to save them to the uttermost that come unto God by him" (Heb. 7:25). Perhaps that which weighs upon you most heavily is a sense of your *past guilt*—you have offended God often, willfully, atrociously, with many aggravations. You feel that all that God's Word says against you is deserved and every threatening that His book utters is your just due. Can so foul a sinner be made clean? I know that the leopard cannot lose its spots nor the Ethiopian change his skin by his own efforts. Is there a power divine that can take away the spots and change your nature? Surely, it already has happened. No sin that you have committed need shut you out of heaven. However damnable your iniquities may have been, there is forgiveness with God that He may be feared. You may have gone to the very edge of hell, but the arm of God's grace is long enough to reach you. You may feel that your tongue is padlocked with blasphemy, your hands bound by acts of atrocious violence, your heart fettered with corruption, your feet chained fast to the satanic blocks of unbelief, your whole self locked up in the bondage of corruption, but there is One so mighty to save that He can set *even you* free. "The blood of Jesus Christ his Son cleanseth us from all sin" (1 John 1:7).

Another person feels he cannot be freed from the *punishment* of sin. He says, "God is just. He must punish sin. It is not possible that the Judge of all the earth should let me go scot-free. Shall I have the same reward with the righteous? After years of disobedience, am I still to be treated as though I had always been a loving child?"

If you place your trust in the blood shedding upon Calvary, there is no need for you to be cast into hell. There is an imperative need that sin should be punished, but there is no need that it should be punished in your person. Christ was punished in your place and suffered the whole of wrath divine, so that there is no fear of your being cast into hell. If you believe, you cannot be punished, for there is no charge against you. Your sin has been laid on Christ, and there can be no punishment exacted upon you, for Christ has already discharged of the whole. God's justice cannot demand two executions for the same offense. Let not Satan provoke you to despair by thoughts of the flames of hell. If your heart says, "Never, never shall I escape," refuse to trust your heart. "God is greater than our heart, and knoweth all things" (1 John 3:20). Believe God's Word and fly to the great Deliverer of liberty. Freedom from punishment is possible through Christ.

I hear one say, "Ah, but if I were saved from these, still I would submit to the *power of sin* again! I have a wolf within my heart hungering after sin that will not be satisfied, though it is glutted with evil. Can I be delivered from it? I have been bound with many resolutions, but sin, like Samson, has snapped them as though they were green branches. I have taken up posts and bars and every other restraint that kept me in, and I have gone back to my old uncleanness. Can I be saved from all this inbred corruption?"

If you believe in the Lord Jesus Christ, that same blood by which sin is pardoned enables man to overcome sin. Those in heaven washed their robes and made them white in His blood, but they have another note in their song—they *overcame* through the blood of the Lamb. They were delivered not only from guilt but also from the power of sin. I cannot tell you that in this life Christ Himself will make you perfectly free from indwelling sin: there will always be some corruption left in you to struggle with, some Canaanite still in the land to exercise your faith and to teach you of the value of the Savior. But the neck of sin shall be under your foot; God shall lead captive the great Goliath of your lust and cut off his head so that he cannot handle the weapons of war again. If the enemy cannot be destroyed, at least his head shall be broken, and he shall never have reigning power over you—you shall be free from sin. How that blessed word *if* sparkles. It may seem but a little star: may it herald the dawning of the sun of righteousness with it—"If the Son therefore shall make you free."

Someone exclaims, "Sir, I am in bondage through *fear of death*. I know that I must close these eyes in the slumbers of the grave, but it is a dread thought that I must stand before God and pass the solemn test. I cannot look into the sepulcher without feeling that it is a horrible place. I cannot think of eternity without remembering the terrors that cluster around it."

Ah, but if the Son makes you free, He will deliver you from the fear of death. When sin is pardoned, the law is satisfied, and when the law is satisfied, death becomes a friend. The strength of sin is the law: the law is fulfilled, therefore the strength of sin is broken. The sting of death is sin: sin is pardoned, therefore death has no longer its sting. If you believe in Christ, you shall never die, in that sense in which you most dread death. That death of which you think is not the Christian's portion. Borne on angels' wings to heaven, up from calamity, imperfection, temptation, and trial, you shall mount, flitting with the wings of a dove far above the clouds of sorrow, leaving this dusky globe behind to enter into the splendors of immortality. You shall not die but shall wake out of this dying world into a life of glory.

I do not think I can bring out the full value of this liberty by merely speaking of the evils that we are delivered *from*. Freedom consists not only in a negative but also in a positive way—we not only are free *from* but also are free *to*. When Jesus Christ sets you free, it includes a sense of privilege—you shall be free to call yourself God's child, you shall be free to say, "Abba, Father," you shall be free to come to His knees with your trials and tell Him all your griefs. You shall be free to plead His promises and to receive the fulfillment of them, too. You shall be free to sit at His table as a well-beloved son, to eat the fatted calf while your Father with you eats, drinks, and is merry. You shall be free to enter into the Church on earth, the mother of us all, free to share in all the blessings that Christ has given to His spouse; and when you die, you shall be free to enter into the rest that remains for the people of God, free to the New Jerusalem that is above, free to her harps of gold and her streets of joy, free to her great banquet that lasts forever, free to the heart of God, to the throne of Christ, and to the blessedness of eternity. How good it is to think that there is a possibility of a freedom to such privileges as these, even for the vilest of the vile!

Look at Paul! No man enters more into the mystery of the gospel than he. Paul was given the freedom to do so: he could comprehend with all saints what are the heights and depths and know the love of Christ that passes knowledge, and yet it is he, it is he who once foamed out threatenings, who drained the blood of the saints. It is Paul who hated Christ and was a persecutor and injurious, and yet he is free from evil, and he is free to all the privileges of the chosen of God. And why not you? Trembling and doubting, come to Him of whom it is said: "He that believeth on him is not condemned" (John 3:18). Oh, that you would be bold and trust Christ.

Beware of a False Liberty

Every good thing is imitated by Satan, who is the master of counterfeits. *Liberty* has been used for the basest of purposes, and men have misnamed the devil's offspring by this angelic term. We have in spiritual matters things called liberty that are not liberty. God deliver us from the false liberty that says, "I am not under the law of God; therefore, I shall live as I like." This is a most blessed truth followed by the most atrocious inference. The Christian is not under the law but is under grace—that is a glorious fact. It is much better to serve God because we love Him than because we are afraid of His wrath. To be under the law is to give God the service of a slave who fears the lash, but to be under grace is to serve God out of pure love for Him.

Oh, to be a child and to give the obedience of a child! But those who infer that not being under the law means that they are free to their own lusts and pleasures are under damnation. They are under a strong delusion to believe this lie. They who can do this must surely have been sometime in Satan's oven to be baked so hard. Why, they must have had their consciences taken out of them. They know God only to provoke Him, and they profess that His love gives them a liberty to rebel.

Refuse legalism, but love the law of God and make it your delight. Abhor all ideas of being saved by good works, but be as full of good works as if you were to be saved by them. Walk in holiness as if your own walking would make you enter into heaven, and then rest in Christ, knowing that nothing of your own can ever open the gate of the Celestial City. When you gather up the doctrines of grace to cheer and comfort you, this false liberty will creep out of the firewood and strike your hand. Shake him into the fire of divine love, and there let the monster be consumed. If we are loved of God with an everlasting love and no more under the law but free from its curse, let us serve God with all our heart's gratitude to Him. "O LORD, truly I am thy servant; I am thy servant, and the son of thine handmaid: thou hast loosed my bonds" (Ps. 116:16).

Another freedom that we must all beware of is that of *hereditary religion*. "Yes, we are the people of God. We have always gone to church, were baptized, and go to the sacrament. Who is free if we are not free? We love God's house and feel a pleasure when we listen to the truth. Who convicts us of sin? We sit as God's people sit, and we hear as God's people hear: sure we are free!"

But a man may think himself free and still be a slave. There are many in this world who dream themselves to be what they are not. Christ must have come to you and shown you your slavery and broken your heart on account of it, or else you are not free. You must have looked to the wounds of Jesus as the only gates of your escape and have seen in His hand the only power that could snap your fetters, or else you are as much slaves of Satan as though you were in the pit itself. Beware, I pray you, of hereditary religion. A man cannot hand down his godliness as he does his possessions, and I cannot receive grace as I may receive lands or gold or silver. "Ye must be born again" (John 3:7). There must be the going up out of Egypt, the leaving the fleshpots and brick kilns, and advancing through the Red Sea of atonement into the wilderness and afterward into the promised rest.

There are many, too, who have the liberty of *natural self-righteousness* and of the *power of the flesh*. They have an unfounded hope of heaven. They have never wronged anyone, never done any mischief in the world, are amiable, generous to the poor; therefore, they feel themselves to be free. They never feel their own inability; they can always pray alike and always sing alike; their confidence never wavers; they believe themselves all right and abide in their confidence. They do not stop to examine: their delusion is too strong, and their comfort is much too precious for them to wish to mar it by looking to its foundation. So they go on, on, on, sound asleep, till one of these days, falling over the awful precipice of ruin, they will wake up where waking will be too late. We know there are some like this in God's house, but they are not God's sons. Just as it was not in the power of Abraham, in the power of the flesh, to beget anything but a slave through Hagar the slave, so we cannot gain God's house through our own efforts. "Cast out the bondwoman and her son: for the son of the bondwoman shall not be heir with the son of the freewoman" (Gal. 4:30). But Isaac, though feeble and tempted and tried and vexed, is never sent out of his father's house—never—he abides there.

Ishmaels attend our churches today. They are very good people in their own way; they do their best, but what is their best? It is the offspring of the flesh, and that which is born of the flesh is of the flesh; consequently, their best endeavors only make them slaves in the house, not sons. Only he who is born by faith according to the promise is the free Isaac and abides in the house. Unless the Spirit of God has given you the spirit of freedom, you will never be free. If the Son of God says to us who are as Ishmael, "I make you free," then are we free indeed, and neither law, justice, heaven, nor hell can bring any argument against us why we should not be free. But do beware of all imaginary freedoms and shun them as you would poison, and God give you to enjoy the glorious liberty of the children of God.

True Freedom Comes Through the Son

No man is set free except as he comes to Christ and takes Him to be his all in all. You may rivet on your fetters by going to the law, to your own good works, to your willings and your prayings and your doings, but you will never be free until you come to Christ. But if you will come to Christ, you will be free this moment from every sort of bondage. None but Jesus can make you free indeed. Real liberty comes from Him only. Think of this liberty for a while. Remember, it is a liberty *righteously bestowed*—Christ has a right to make men free. If I should set a slave free who belongs to his master, he might run for a time; but since I had not the power to legally emancipate the man, he would be dragged back again. But the law is on Christ's side. Christ has such power in heaven and earth committed to Him that if He says to the sinner, "You are free," free he is before high heaven. Before God's great judgment seat you can plead the word of Jesus and you shall be delivered.

Consider as well *how dearly this freedom was purchased*. Christ speaks it by His power, but He still bought it by His blood. He makes you free, but it is by His own bonds. You may go clear, because He bore your burden. See Him bear His agony, dragged to Pilate's hall, bound, whipped like a common felon, scourged like a murderer, and dragged away by hellhounds through the streets, fastened by those cruel fetters that went through His flesh, to the accursed wood. See Him yielding up His liberty to the dungeon of death; there the mighty one sleeps in Joseph of Arimathea's tomb.

Dearly did He purchase with His own bondage the liberty that He so freely gives. But though dearly purchased, let us take up that key note—*He freely gives it*. Jesus asks nothing of us as a preparation for this liberty. He finds us sitting in sackcloth and ashes and bids us put on the beautiful array of freedom. He discovers us in a darkness that may be felt, sitting in the valley of the shadow of death, and He brings the true light in His hand and turns our midnight into blazing noon, and all without our help, without our merit, and at first without our will. Christ died not for the righteous but for the ungodly, and His message is grace, pure grace, undiluted by a single condition or requisition that God might make of man. Just as you are, trust your soul with Christ, and though there is in you no speck of that which is good, He will save you and give you perfect liberty. Dearly has He brought it, but freely does He give it, even the faith by which we receive is the gift of God.

It is a liberty that may be *instantaneously received*. The captive goes first through one door and then another, and perhaps a hundred keys must grate in the wards of the lock before he feels the cool fresh air gladdening his face. But it is not so with the man who believes. The moment you believe, you are free. You may have been chained at a thousand points, but the instant you believe in Christ, you are unfettered and free as the bird of the air. No more free is the eagle that mounts to his rocky eyrie and afterward outsoars the clouds—even he, the bird of God, is not more unfettered than the soul that Christ has delivered. Cut are the cords, and in an instant you are free, and upward you mount to God. He can make you say, "Abba, Father," with your whole heart, though up to this day you may have been of your father the devil, and his works you have done. When once the shower of Jesus' grace falls on the heart, even the desert is turned to green grass and blossoms like the garden of the Lord, and that in a moment. You who have given yourself up in despair, you who have written your own condemnation, you who have made a league with death and a covenant with hell, I charge you that my Lord and Master has broken the chains to set you free and can make you free with one blow.

Mark, that if this is done, it is *done forever*. When Christ sets free, no chains can bind again. Let the Master say to you, "Captive, I have set you free." Come on, you fiends of the pit! Mightier is He who is for us than all they who are against us. Come on temptations of the world, but if the Lord is on our side, whom shall we fear? If He is our defense, who shall be our destruction? Come on, you foul corruptions that work on my own deceitful heart, but He who has begun a good work in me will carry it on and perfect it to the end. Gather all your hosts together, you who are the foes of God and the enemies of man, and come at once with concentrated fury and with hellish might against my spirit. But if God acquits sinners, who is he that condemns? Who shall separate us from the love of God that is in Christ Jesus our Lord (Rom. 8:35)? The black stream of death shall never wash out the mark of Christian liberty. That skeleton monarch bears no yoke that he can put upon a believer's neck. We will shout victory when we are neck deep among the last billows and grapple with the king upon the pale horse. We will throw the rider and win the victory in the last struggle, according as it is written: "But thanks be to God, which giveth us the victory through our Lord Jesus Christ" (1 Cor. 15:57). We refuse the yoke of Satan and will overcome his power as Christ overcame it in the days gone by. Let those who will bend and crouch at the foot of the world's monarch, but as for those whom God has made free, they claim to think, to believe, to act, and to be as their divine instinct commands them and the Spirit of God enables them. "Where the Spirit of the Lord is, there is liberty" (2 Cor. 3:17).

If you are free, remember that *you have changed your place of dwelling*, for the slave and the son do not sleep in the same room of the house. The things that satisfied you when a slave will not satisfy you now. You wear a garment that the slave may never wear, and you feel an instinct within that the slave can never feel. There is an "Abba, Father," cry in you, that was not there once. Is it not so?

If you are free, *you live not as you once did*. You do not go to the slave's work, you do not now have to toil and sweat to earn the wages of sin which is death, but now as a son serves his father, you do a son's work and expect to receive a son's reward, for the gift of God is eternal life through Jesus Christ our Lord. If you are free, *you are thinking about setting others free*; and if you have no zeal for the emancipation of others, you are a slave yourself. If you are free, *you hate all sorts of chains*, all sorts of sin, and you will never willingly put on the fetters anymore. You live each day, crying to Him who made you free at first to hold you up that you fall not into the snare. If you are free, this is not the world to you; this is the land of slaves; this is the world of bondage. If you are free, your heart has gone to heaven, the land of the free. If you are free, your spirit is longing for the time when you shall see the great Liberator face-to-face. If you are free, you will wait your time until He calls you and says, "Friend, come up beside Me," and you will fearlessly mount to the upper spheres, and death and sin shall be no hindrance to your advent to His glory.

If you long for liberty, you shall have it. When you seek for liberty as for hidden treasure and pant for it as the deer for the waterbrook, God will not deny you. "Ask, and it shall be given you; seek, and ye shall find; knock, and it shall be opened unto you" (Matt. 7:7).

*N*ote another singular combination in the Lamb. He is called "a little lamb," for the diminutive is used in the Greek, but yet how great He is! In Jesus, as a Lamb, we see great tenderness and exceeding familiarity with His people. He is not the object of dread; there is about Him nothing like "stand away, for I am too holy to be approached." A lamb is the most approachable of beings. Yet there is about the little Lamb an exceeding majesty. The elders no sooner saw Him and they fell down in worship, crying, "Worthy is the Lamb" (Rev. 5:12). Every creature worshiped Him, saying, "Blessing, and honour, and glory, and power, be unto him that sitteth upon the throne, and unto the Lamb for ever and ever" (vs. 13). He is so great that the heavens cannot contain Him, yet He becomes so little that He dwells in humble hearts. He is so glorious that the seraphim veil their faces in His presence, yet so condescending as to become bone of our bone and flesh of our flesh. What a wonderful combination of mercy and majesty, grace and glory! Never divide what God has joined together: do not speak of our Lord Jesus Christ, as some do, with irreverent familiarity, but at the same time, do not think of Him as some great Lord for whom we must feel a slavish dread. Jesus is your next of kin, a brother born for adversity, and yet He is your God and your Lord. Let love and awe keep the watches of your soul!

Chapter Seven

The Lamb in Glory

And I beheld, and, lo, in the midst of the throne and of the four beasts, and in the midst of the elders, stood a Lamb as it had been slain, having seven horns and seven eyes, which are the seven Spirits of God sent forth into all the earth. And he came and took the book out of the right hand of him that sat upon the throne
—Revelation 5:6–7.

THE APOSTLE JOHN had long known the Lord Jesus as the Lamb. That was his first view of Him, when John the Baptist, pointing to Jesus, said, "Behold the Lamb of God, which taketh away the sin of the world" (John 1:29). He had been very familiar with this blessed person, having often laid his head upon His bosom, feeling that this tender goodness of the Savior proved Him to be in nature gentle as a lamb. John had beheld Jesus when He was brought "as a lamb to the slaughter" (Isa. 53:7), so that the idea was indelibly fixed upon his mind that Jesus, the Christ, was the Lamb of God. John knew that Jesus was the appointed sacrifice, set forth in the morning and evening Lamb and in the Paschal Lamb, by whose blood Israel was redeemed from death. In his last days, the beloved disciple was to see this same Christ, under the same figure of a lamb, as the great revealer of secrets, the expounder of the mind of God, the taker of the sealed book, and the one who would loose the seals that bound up the mysterious purposes of God toward the children of men. I pray that we may have on this earth a clear and constant sight of the sin-bearing Lamb, and then, in the world of glory to come, we shall behold Him in the midst of the throne and the living creatures and the elders.

The appearance of this Lamb at the particular moment described by John was exceedingly suitable. Our Lord usually appears when all other hope disappears. Concerning the wine-press of wrath, it is He who says, "I have trodden the winepress alone; and of the people there was none with me" (Isa. 63:3). In the instance before us, the strong angel had proclaimed, "Who is worthy to open the book, and to loose the seals thereof?" (Rev. 5:2). And there was no response from heaven or earth or hell. No man was able to open the book, neither to look within it. The divine decrees must remain forever sealed in mystery unless the once slain Mediator shall take them from the hand of God and open them to the sons of men. When no one could do this, John wept much. At that grave moment, the Lamb appeared. When there is utter failure everywhere else, then in Him is our help found.

If there could have been found another bearer of sin, would the Father have given His Son to die? Had any other been able to unfold the secret designs of God, would He not have appeared at the angel's challenge? But He who came to take away the sin of the world now appears to take away the seals that bind up the eternal purposes. O Lamb of God, You are able to do what none beside may venture to attempt! You come forth when no one else is to be found. Remember, the next time you are in trouble, that when no man can comfort or save, you may expect the Lord, the ever sympathetic Lamb of God, to appear on your behalf.

Before the Lamb appeared, John's weeping eyes were seen by the Lamb of God. Certain ministers of this present age who make so little of the doctrine of substitutionary sacrifice would have been of another mind if they had known more contrition of heart and exercise of the soul. Eyes washed by repentance are best able to see those blessed truths that shine forth from our incarnate God. Free grace and dying love are most appreciated by the mourners in Zion. If tears are good for the eyes, the Lord sends us to be weepers and leads us around Bochim to Bethel as He did the Israelites when they had sinned (Jud. 2:1–5). I have heard the old proverb, "There is no going to heaven but by the Weeping Cross," and there seems no way of even seeing heaven and the heavenly One except by eyes that have wept. Weeping makes the eyes quick to see if there is any hope, and while it dims them to all false confidences, it makes them sensitive to the faintest beam of divine light. "They looked unto him, and were lightened: and their faces were not ashamed" (Ps. 34:5). Those who have laid eternal matters to heart so much as to weep over their own need and that of their fellow men shall be the first to see in the Lamb of God the answer to their desires.

Yet observe that even in this case, human instrumentality was permitted, for it is written, "And one of the elders saith unto me, Weep not" (Rev. 5:5). John the apostle was greater than an elder. Among them who are born of men, in the Church of God we put none before John, who leaned his head upon his Master's bosom; and yet a mere elder of the Church reproves and instructs the beloved apostle! He cheers John with the news that the Lion of the tribe of Judah had prevailed to open the book and to loose the seven seals. The greatest man in the Church may be under obligations to the least: a preacher may be taught by a convert; an elder may be instructed by a child. Oh, that we might be always willing to learn—to learn from anyone, however lowly! Assuredly, we shall be teachable if we have the tenderness of heart that shows itself in weeping. This will make our own souls like waxen tablets, upon which the finger of truth may readily inscribe its teaching. God grant us this preparation of heart!

May we come in a teachable spirit to the text, and may the Lord open our eyes to see and learn with John! It is no small favor that we have the record of the vision. Does not the Lord intend us to be partakers in it? The vision is that of a Lamb, a Lamb that is to open the book of God's secret purposes. The teaching of the passage is that the Lord Jesus, in His sacrificial character, is the most prominent object in the heavenly world. So far from substitution being done with and laid aside as a temporary expedient, it remains the object of universal wonder and adoration. He who became a Lamb that He might take away the sin of the world is not ashamed of His humiliation but still manifests it to adoring myriads and is, for that very reason, the very object of their enthusiastic worship. They worship the Lamb even as they worship Him who sits upon the throne; and they say, "Worthy is the Lamb" (Rev. 5:12), because He was slain and redeemed His people by His blood. His atoning sacrifice is the great reason for their deepest reverence and their highest adoration.

Jesus' Sacrificial Character

Jesus in heaven appears in His sacrificial character, and I would note that this character is enhanced by other conspicuous points. Its glory is not diminished but enhanced by all the rest of our Lord's character: the attributes, achievements, and offices of our Lord all concentrate their glory in His sacrificial character, and all unite in making it a theme for loving wonder.

We read that *He is the Lion of the tribe of Judah*, by which is signified the dignity of His office as King and the majesty of His person as Lord. The lion is at home in the fight, and "the LORD is a man of war: the LORD is his name" (Exod. 15:3). Like a lion, He is courageous, though He is like a lamb for tenderness, yet not in timidity. He is terrible as a lion: "who shall rouse him up?" (Gen. 49:9). If any come in contact with Him, let them beware, for as He is courageous, so is He full of force and altogether irresistible in might. He has the lion's heart and the lion's strength, and He comes forth conquering and to conquer. This is what makes it the more wonderful that He should become a lamb and yield Himself up to the indignities of the cross. Oh, wonder, wonder, wonder, that the Lion of Judah, the offshoot of David's royal house, should become as a lamb led forth to the slaughter!

Further, it is clear that *He is a champion*: "the Lion of the tribe of Juda, the Root of David, hath prevailed" (Rev. 5:5). What was asked for was worthiness, not only in the sense of holiness but also in the sense of valor. One is reminded of a legend of the Crusades. A fine castle and estate awaited the return of the lawful heir. He alone could sound the horn that hung at the castle gate, but he who could make it yield a blast would be one who had come home victorious from many a bloody fray. So here, no man in earth or heaven had valor and renown enough to be worthy to take the mystic roll out of the hand of the Eternal. Our champion was worthy. What battles He had fought! What feats of prowess He had performed! He had overthrown sin; He had met face-to-face the prince of darkness and overcome him in the wilderness.

Yes, Jesus had conquered death and bearded that lion in his den and had entered the dungeon of the sepulcher and torn its bars away. Thus, He was worthy, in the sense of valor, on returning from the far country to be owned as the Father's glorious Son, heaven's hero, and so to take the book and loose the seals. The brilliance of His victories does not diminish our delight in Him as the

Lamb. Far otherwise, for He won these triumphs as the Lamb by gentleness and suffering and sacrifice. He won His battles by meekness and patience before unknown. The more of a conqueror He is, the more astounding is it that He should win by humiliation and death. Never tolerate low thoughts of Christ! Think of Him more and more, as did Mary when she sang, "My soul doth magnify the Lord, and my spirit hath rejoiced in God my Saviour" (Luke 1:46–47). Make your thought of Him great, and then add to your reverent thoughts the reflection that still He looks like a lamb that has been slain. His prowess and His lionlike qualities do but set forth more vividly the tender, lowly, condescending relationship in which He stands to us as the Lamb of our redemption.

In this wonderful vision we see Jesus as *the familiar of God*. He it was who, without hesitation, advanced to the burning throne and took the book out of the right hand of Him who sat upon it. He was at home there: He who counted it not robbery to be equal with God (Phil. 2:6). He is very God of very God, to be extolled with equal honor with that which is given to the Lord God Almighty. He advances to the throne, takes the book, communes with Jehovah, accepts the divine challenge of love, and unseals the mysterious purposes of His glorious Father. To Him there is no danger in a close approach to the infinite glory, for that glory is His own. Now, it is He who thus stood on familiar terms with God who also stood in our place and bore for us the penalty of sin. He who is greater than the greatest and higher than the highest became lower than the lowest, that He might save to the uttermost those who come to God by Him. He who is Lord of all stooped under all the load and burden of sin. Fall down on your face and worship the Lamb, for though He became obedient unto death, He is God over all, blessed forever, the Beloved of the Father.

We also observe that *He is the prophet of God*. He it was who had the seven eyes to see all things and discern all mysteries (Rev. 5:6). He it is who opened the seven seals and thus unfolded the parts of the Book one after another, not merely that they might be read but that they might be actually fulfilled; and yet He had been our substitute. Jesus explains everything: the Lamb is the one before whom nothing is secret. He foresaw His own sufferings, which came not upon Him as a surprise. Since then He has not been ignorant of our unworthiness or of the treachery of our hearts. He knows all about us; He knows what we cost Him, and He knows how we have repaid Him. With all that knowledge of God and of man, He is not ashamed to call us brethren, nor does He reject that truth so simple, yet so full of hope to us, that He is our sacrifice and our substitute.

Our Lord always was, and is now, *acknowledged to be Lord and God*. All the Church worships Him; all the myriads of angels cry aloud in praises to Him; and to Him every creature bows, of things in heaven and things on earth and things that are under the earth (Rev. 5:13). When you call Him King of kings and Lord of lords, lofty as these titles are, they fall far below His glory and majesty. If we all stood up with all the billions of the human race and with one voice lifted up a shout of praise to Him, loud as the noise of many waters and as great thunders, yet would our highest honors scarcely reach the lowest step of His all glorious throne. Yet, in the glory of His deity, He disdains not to appear as the Lamb that has been slain. This still is His chosen character. I have heard of a great warrior who, on the anniversary of his most renowned victory, would always put on the coat in which he fought the fight, adorned, as it was, with marks of shot. I understand his choice. Our Lord today, and every day, wears still the human flesh in which He overthrew our enemies, and He appears as one who has but newly died, since by death He overcame the devil. Always and forever He is the Lamb. Even as God's prophet and revealer, He remains the Lamb. When you shall see Him at the last, you shall say, "I beheld, and, lo, in the midst of the throne…a Lamb as it had been slain" (vs. 6).

Write, then, the passion of your Lord upon the tablets of your hearts, and let no one erase the treasured memory. Think of Him mainly and chiefly as the sacrifice for sin. Set the atonement in the midst of your mind and let it tinge and color all your thoughts and beliefs. Jesus bleeding and dying in your place must be to you as the sun in your sky.

In This Character Jesus Is the Center of All

"In the midst of the throne and of the four beasts, and in the midst of the elders, stood a Lamb" (vs. 6). The Lamb is the center of the wonderful circle that makes up the fellowship of heaven.

From Him, as a standpoint, all things are seen in their places. Looking up at the planets from this earth, it is difficult to comprehend their motions—progressive, retrograde, or standing still; but the angel in the sun sees all the planets marching in due course and circling about the center of their system. Standing where you are upon this earth and within human range of opinion, you cannot see all things correctly until you come to Jesus, and then you see all things from the center. The man who knows the incarnate God, slain for human sins, stands in the center of truth. Now he sees God in His place, man in his place, angels in their place, lost souls in their place, and the saved ones in their place. Know Him whom to know is life eternal, and you are in the position of vantage from which you may rightly judge all things. In Christ you are in the right position to understand the past, the present, and the future. The deep mysteries of eternity, and even the secrets of the Lord, are all with you when once you are with Jesus. Think of this and make the Lamb your central thought—the soul of your soul, the heart of your heart's best life.

The Lamb, being in the midst, signifies also that *in Him they all meet in One*. I would speak cautiously, but I venture to say that Christ is the summing up of all existence. Seek you Godhead? There it is. Seek you manhood? There it is. Wish you the spiritual? There it is in His human soul. Desire you the material? There it is in His human body. Our Lord has gathered up the ends of all things and bound them into one. You cannot conceive what God is, but Christ is God. If you dive down into materialism, which for many is a millstone of the soul, yet in Jesus you find materialism, refined and elevated and brought into union with the divine nature. In Jesus all lines meet, and from Him they radiate to all the points of being. Would you meet God? Go to Christ. Would you be in fellowship with all believers? Go to Christ. Would you feel tenderness toward all that God has made? Go to Christ, for "of him, and through him, and to him, are all things" (Rom. 11:36). What a Lord is ours! What a glorious being the Lamb, for it is only as the Lamb that this is true of Him! View Him only as God, and there is no such meeting with man. View Him as being only man, and then He is far from the center. But behold Him as God and man, and the Lamb of God, and then you see in Him the place of rest for all things.

Being in the center, *to Him they all look*. Can you think for a moment how the Lord God looks upon His Only Begotten? When Jehovah looks on Jesus, it is with an altogether indescribable delight. He says, "This is my beloved Son, in whom I am well pleased" (Matt. 3:17). When He thinks of the passion through which His Son passed and the death that He accomplished at Jerusalem, all the infinite heart of God flows high and strong toward His Best-Beloved. The Father has rest in His Son as He has nowhere else. His delight is in Jesus; indeed, He has so much delight in Him that for His sake He takes delight in His people. As the Father's eyes are always on Jesus, so are the eyes of the living creatures and the elders who represent the Church in its divine life and the Church in its human life. All who have been washed in Jesus' blood perpetually contemplate His beauties. What is there in heaven that can compare with the adorable person of Him by whom they were redeemed? All angels look that way, also, waiting His august commands. Are they not all ministering spirits, whom He sends forth to minister to His people? All the forces of nature wait for the call of Jesus; all the powers of providence look to Him for direction. He is the focus of all attention, the center of all observation throughout the plains of heaven. This, remember, is "the Lamb." Not as king or prophet chiefly but preeminently as "the Lamb" is Jesus the center of all reverence and love and thought in the glory above.

Around the throne, *all seem to rally to the Lamb as guards to a king*. It is for the Lamb that the Father acts: He glorifies His Son. The Holy Spirit also glorifies Christ. All the divine purposes run that way. The chief work of God is to make Jesus the firstborn among many brethren. This is the model to which the Creator works in fashioning the vessels of grace: He has made Jesus Alpha and Omega, the beginning and the end. All things ordained of the Father work toward Christ as their center; and so stand all the redeemed and all the angels waiting about the Lord, as swelling His glory and manifesting His praise. If anything could enter the minds of heavenly beings that would contribute to lift Jesus higher, it would be their heaven to speed throughout space to carry it out. He dwells as a King in His central pavilion, and this is the joy of the host: the King is in the midst of them.

Beloved, is it so? Is Jesus the center of the whole heavenly family? Shall He not be the center of our Church life? Will we not think most of Him—much more of Him than of Paul or Apollos or Peter or any others who might divide us? Christ is the center, not a doctrine or a mode of ordinance, but the Lamb alone. Shall we not always delight in Him and watch to see how we can magnify His glorious name? Shall He not be also the center of our ministry? What shall we preach about except Christ! Take that subject away from me, and I am done. These many years I have preached nothing else but that dear name, and if that is to be dishonored, all my spiritual wealth is gone. After all these years my speech has become like the harp of Anacreaon, which would resound love alone. It is so with my ministry: with Christ and Christ alone am I at home. No string of my soul will vibrate to the touch of progressive theology. My harp is silent to the strange fingers of modern thought, evolution, and new divinity. But to Christ and Christ alone it answers with all the music of which it is capable.

Beloved, is it so with you? In teaching your children, in your life at home, in your dealings with the world, is Jesus the center of your aim and labor? Does His love fill your heart? In the old Napoleon's days, a soldier was wounded by a bullet, and the doctor probed deep to find it. The man cried out, "Doctor, mind what you are doing! A little deeper, and you will touch the Emperor." The Emperor was on that soldier's heart. Truly, if they search deep in our life, they will find Christ engraven on our heart.

In This Character the Lamb Exhibits Peculiar Marks

Note well the words "stood a Lamb as it had been slain." "Stood," here is a posture of *life*; "as it had been slain," here is the memorial of *death*. Our view of Jesus should be twofold: we should see His death and His life; we shall never receive a whole Christ in any other way. If you see Him only on the cross, you behold the power of His death; but He is not now upon the cross; He is risen, He forever lives to make intercession for us, and we need to know the power of His life. We see Him as a Lamb "as it had been slain," but we worship Him as One who "liveth for ever and ever." Carry these two things with you as one: a slain Christ, a living Christ. We adore the Crucified One upon the throne of God. We believe in Him as bleeding and pleading: we see Him slain and behold Him reign. Both of these are our joy; neither one more than the other, but each in its own place. Thus, as you look at the Lamb, you begin to sing, "Thou art He who lives, and was dead, and is alive forevermore." The mark of our Savior is life through death, and death slain by death.

Note, next, another singular combination in the Lamb. He is called "a little lamb," for the diminutive is used in the Greek, but yet how great He is! In Jesus, as a Lamb, we see great tenderness and exceeding familiarity with His people. He is not the object of dread; there is about Him nothing like "stand away, for I am too holy to be approached." A lamb is the most approachable of beings. Yet there is about the little Lamb an exceeding majesty. The elders no sooner saw Him and they fell down in worship, crying, "Worthy is the Lamb" (Rev. 5:12). Every creature worshiped Him, saying, "Blessing, and honour, and glory, and power, be unto him that sitteth upon the throne, and unto the Lamb for ever and ever" (vs. 13). He is so great that the heavens cannot contain Him, yet He becomes so little that He dwells in humble hearts. He is so glorious that the seraphim veil their faces in His presence, yet so condescending as to become bone of our bone and flesh of our flesh. What a wonderful combination of *mercy and majesty*, grace and glory! Never divide what God has joined together: do not speak of our Lord Jesus Christ, as some do, with irreverent familiarity, but at the same time, do not think of Him as some great Lord for whom we must feel a slavish dread. Jesus is your next of kin, a brother born for adversity, and yet He is your God and your Lord. Let love and awe keep the watches of your soul!

Further, let us look at the peculiar marks of Him, and we see that He has *seven horns and seven eyes*. His power is equal to His vigilance, and these are equal to all the emergencies brought about by the opening of the seven seals of the book. When plagues break forth, who is to defend us? Behold the seven horns. If the unexpected occurs, who is to forewarn us? Behold the seven eyes.

Every now and then some foolish person brings out a pamphlet stuffed with horrors that are going to happen in a year or two. The whole of it is absolutely worthless, but still, if it were true as the prophecy mongers tell us, we are not afraid. The Lamb has seven horns and will meet every difficulty by His own power, having already foreseen it by His own wisdom. The Lamb is the answer to the enigma of providence. Providence is a riddle, but Jesus explains it all. During the first centuries, the Church of God was given up to martyrdom: every possible torment and torture was exercised upon the followers of Christ. What could be God's meaning in all this? What but the glory of the Lamb? And now, today, the Lord seems to leave His Church to wander into all kinds of errors: false doctrines are, in some places, fearfully paramount. What does this mean? I do not know, but the Lamb knows, for He sees with seven eyes. As a Lamb, as our Savior, God and man, He understands all and has the clues of all labyrinths in His hands. He has power to meet every difficulty and wisdom to see through every embarrassment. We should cast out fear and give ourselves wholly up to worship.

The Lamb also works to perfection in nature and in providence; for with Him are "the seven Spirits of God sent into all the earth." This refers not merely to the saving power of the Spirit that is sent forth to the elect, but to those powers and forces that operate upon all the earth. The power of gravity, the energy of life, the forces of electricity, and the like are all forms of the power of God. A law of nature is nothing but our observation of the usual way in which God operates in the world. A law in itself has no power: law is but the usual course of God's action. All the Godhead's omnipotence dwells in the Lord: He is the Lord God Almighty. We cannot put the atonement into a secondary place, for our atoning sacrifice has all the seven Spirits of God. Jesus is able to save to the uttermost them that come to God by Him. Let us come to God by Him. He has the power to cope with the future, whatever it may be. Let us secure our souls against all threatening dangers, committing ourselves to His keeping.

How I wish that I had the power to set before you the Lamb as He is! My words are like holding a candle to the sun. I am grateful that my Lord does not snuff me out. Perhaps my candle may show some prisoner to the door, and when he has once passed it, he will behold the sun in its strength. Glory be to Him who is so great, so glorious, and yet still the Lamb slain for sinners, whose wounds in effect continually bleed for our life, whose finished work is the perpetual source of all our safety and our joy.

In This Character the Lamb Is Universally Adored

Before He opened one of the seals, this worship commenced. When He had taken the book, the four living creatures and the elders fell down before the Lamb and sang a new song: "Thou art worthy to take the book" (Rev. 5:8–9). While yet the book is closed, we worship Him. We trust Him where we cannot trace Him. Before He begins His work as the revealing Mediator, the Church adores Him for His work as a sacrifice. Jesus our Lord is worshiped not so much for what benefits He will confer as for Himself. As the Lamb slain He is the object of heavenly reverence. Many will reverence

Him when He comes in His second advent. Every knee shall bow in that day, but that is not the worship that He accepts or that proves the offerer to be saved. You must worship Him as a sacrifice as the "despised and rejected of men" (Isa. 53:3). You must reverence Him while others ridicule Him, trust His blood while others turn from it with disdain, and so be with Him in His humiliation.

That adoration *begins with the Church of God*. The Church of God, in all its phases, adores the Lamb. If you view the Church of God as a divine creation, the embodiment of the Spirit of God, then the living creatures fall down before the Lamb. No God-begotten life is too high to refuse obeisance to the Lord God. Look at the Church on its human side and you see the twenty-four elders falling down and worshiping. Well may the whole company of redeemed men worship the Mediator, since in Him our manhood is greatly exalted! Was ever our nature so exalted as it is now that Christ is made Head over all things to His Church? Now we are nearest to God, for between man and God no creature intervenes: Emmanuel—God with us—has joined us in one. Man is next to the deity, with Jesus only in between, not to divide but to unite. The Lord in Christ Jesus has made us to have dominion over all the works of His hands; He has put all things under our feet. O Lord our God, how excellent is Your name in all the earth!

The Lord is adored by the Church in all forms of worship. The Church worships Him in prayer, for the vials full of sweet odors are the prayers of saints. It worships Him in praise with a new song and with the postures of lowliest reverence.

But, beloved, not only is the Lamb worshiped by the Church, but also *He is worshiped by the angels*. What a wonderful gathering together of certain legions of the Lord's hosts we have before us in this chapter! "Ten thousand times ten thousand, and thousands of thousands" (Rev. 5:11). Their company cannot be enumerated in human arithmetic. With perfect unanimity that united in the hallowed worship, the angels shout together, "Worthy is the Lamb that was slain" (vs. 12).

Nay, it is not merely the Church and angels, but *all creation*, east, west, north, south, highest, lowest, all adore Him. All life, all space, all time, immensity, eternity, all these become one mouth for song, and the song is "Worthy is the Lamb."

Now, if this is all true, cannot you trust the Lamb here below? O you who are burdened with sin, here is your deliverance: come to the sin-bearing Lamb. You who are perplexed in doubts, here is your guide: the Lamb can open the sealed books for you. You who have lost your comfort, come back to the Lamb and put your trust in Him. You who are hungering for heavenly food, come to the Lamb, for He shall feed you. The Lamb, the Lamb, the little bleeding Lamb: may this be the song upon the standard of the Church of God. Set that as the emblem at the front and march boldly on to victory, and then, O Lamb of God, grant us Your peace!

The fact that Jesus does now reign is in the text: "He must reign, till he hath put all enemies under his feet." Jesus is reigning even now in heaven. There, no shame can approach Him, and no scorn can even be whispered at His feet. He reigns there with undisputed sway; it would not be possible for me to fully depict the royal state in which Emmanuel sits enthroned above, but I would like your faith to endeavor to realize it. You may even venture to call on your sanctified imagination to aid you to sketch the scene where He reigns in glory. There is no province of the celestial domain that does not own His sway, and not one individual of all the happy tribes that dwell in glory but is glad to call Him King. The holy angels, whom He has made to be as flames of fire, delight to do His commandments, hearkening to the voice of His Word. All the various orders of cherubim and seraphim yield Him their loyal homage, and all the angels and principalities and powers in the heavenly places own Him as their Lord forever. His redeemed occupy the most honorable place in heaven; nearest to the throne you will find the twenty-four elders, the representatives of the Church; and then, in the outer ring, stand the angels worshiping and adoring; and all the redeemed spirits—as well they may, since they owe their glory to His blood—call Jesus their Lord and King. He is no servant here; He washes no disciple's feet there; He goes not to Pilate's hall to be judged. Absolute and supreme is He—King of kings, for they are all kings whom He has redeemed, and Lord of lords, for they are all lordly ones over whom He reigns–and He occupies the highest seat amid the splendors of the celestial realm.

Chapter Eight

He Must Reign

For he must reign, till he hath put all enemies under his feet
—1 Corinthians 15:25.

"HE MUST REIGN." There was another "must" that His disciples were slow to learn. Very much of our Lord's teaching to His apostles was concerning the necessity that He must suffer. That doctrine seemed so strange to them that at first they could hardly catch the idea. When they perceived that Christ really meant it, they could not bear the thought. Peter even began to rebuke his Lord, but Jesus sharply stopped him. The notion that Christ must suffer could not be drilled into the apostles, and do you wonder? If you had lived with the dear and blessed Lord and had seen the perfection of His character, the liberality of His gifts, and the tenderness of His heart, and if you had known, as they did to a certain level, the glory of His nature and the marvel of His person, could you have endured the thought that He must be despitefully used, spit upon, and nailed like a felon to a cross? Even Christ Himself might have found it difficult to get that thought into your mind. It was such a cruel "must" that He must die. Even after He had died and all the prophecies concerning His death had been fulfilled, it was still a bewilderment to His disciples. The two, who

103

walked to Emmaus with Christ, were in a daze concerning it, and He had to say to them, "O fools, and slow of heart to believe all that the prophets have spoken: Ought not Christ to have suffered these things, and to enter into his glory?" (Luke 24:25–26).

The first "must" cost the people of God much before they learned it, but we know very well that the price of pardon for us was Christ's suffering and death. We understand that there was no other way to access for us but by the atonement—no other method by which the lost inheritance could come back except by that ransom price that was found in the pierced heart of Christ. And now there is another "must" which, I think, is almost as difficult for us to learn. The shadow of the cross has fallen upon us, and we live so much in its shade that it is not easy for us to catch the gleam of that necessity that comes from His throne: "He must reign."

The cross, too, is on our shoulder. It is not merely that we live in the shadow of the cross, but the burden of the cross has to be cheerfully endured from day to day; as we bear it, it is not easy for us to feel that "He must reign." When you preach but no one gives heed to your message, when you teach but the children will not yield their hearts to the Lord, when you meet with hard and cold hearts in every place that draw not even beneath the sunbeams of the love of Jesus, you are very apt to say that it does not appear that "He must reign." The long rebellion against Jehovah still continues, the dread revolt against the majesty of heaven seems as if it will never end, and we sometimes fear that the treason will last on to all eternity.

It appears impossible that the crucified Christ shall yet be the universal Conqueror, that the man of Nazareth will yet mount His white horse and lead His conquering armies to the last charge and to final victory; and yet, as surely as it was true that He must suffer, so surely "He must reign." And it necessitates that we open our hearts to this predestined necessity ordained of the Most High. Jesus must reign; His defeat is not to be thought for a moment. Delay there may be, but the victory must come. Let heaven ring with the anticipation of it; let earth resound with the prophecy of it; let hell's darkest cavern hear the tidings of that imperative necessity: "He must reign." And let every believer feel revived and quickened by the joyful sound that He who had to die must surely reign.

Jesus Reigns Now
as a Prelude to Its Greater Fulfillment

The fact that Jesus does now reign is in the text: "He must reign, *till* he hath put all enemies under his feet." *Jesus is reigning even now in heaven.* There, no shame can approach Him, and no scorn can even be whispered at His feet. He reigns there with undisputed sway; it would not be possible for me to fully depict the royal state in which Emmanuel sits enthroned above, but I would like your faith to endeavor to realize it. You may even venture to call on your sanctified imagination to aid you to sketch the scene where He reigns in glory. There is no province of the celestial domain that does not own His sway, and not one individual of all the happy tribes that dwell in glory but is glad to call Him King. The holy angels, whom He has made to be as flames of fire, delight to do His commandments, hearkening to the voice of His Word. All the various orders of cherubim and seraphim yield Him their loyal homage, and all the angels and principalities and powers in the heavenly places own Him as their Lord forever. His redeemed occupy the most honorable place in heaven; nearest to the throne you will find the twenty-four elders, the representatives of the Church; and then, in the outer ring, stand the angels worshiping and adoring; and all the redeemed spirits—as well they may, since they owe their glory to His blood—call Jesus their Lord and King. He is no servant here; He washes no disciple's feet there; He goes not to Pilate's hall to be judged. Absolute and supreme is He—King of kings, for they are all kings whom He has redeemed, and Lord of lords, for they are all lordly ones over whom He reigns–and He occupies the highest seat amid the splendors of the celestial realm.

But do not imagine that Christ's reign is limited to those gates of pearl and streets of shining gold. Far from it, for *Jesus reigns today on earth.* We gather and sing, "Crown Him Lord of all," and in our inmost souls, we are wishing Him all honor and glory and delightedly confessing our allegiance to Him. O Jesus, You have still on earth myriads whose highest joy is found in Your name and who find their heaven on earth as they think of You. In Your Church, You are still Lord and Master, and if there are churches that revolt against You and play the harlot, You have Your chaste spouse still, and You reign over her in undisputed sovereignty.

Nor is Christ's kingdom limited to the Church in heaven and the Church on earth, for *He reigns today over all things.* "All power is given unto me in heaven and in earth" (Matt. 28:18). Providence is at the disposal of the Nazarene. Let those doubt it who will, but we believe that every event that happens—political, national, social, domestic—is overruled by Him for the accomplishment of the grand designs of mercy that He has for His own elect. Just as Joseph reigned in Egypt and all had to come to him for food in the time of famine, so does Jesus reign in the courts of earth for the good of His people. His cause must prosper, for He is always at the helm. Even where confusion seems to rule, He is everywhere King, putting a bit into the mouth of the tempest and riding upon the wings of the wind. Just as the seas owned His presence when He was here incarnate, so do they own His presence now. And just as the earth then felt His tread, so does she feel it now; but it is no more the weary tramp of the Son of Man, but the majestic footfall of the Son of God. He rules everywhere. "In his hand are the deep places of the earth: the strength of the hills is his also. The sea is his, and he made it: and his hands formed the dry land" (Ps. 95:4–5).

He reigns, too, even in hell itself. The devils bite their iron bonds in grim despair because He reigns. They tried to make this earth their own, but now they know the prowess, the strong arm, and the valiant heart of Jesus Christ, the Son of the Highest, and they must do His bidding. "Hitherto shalt thou come, but no further" (Job 38:11) is His command to the spirits grim and fierce, and they are compelled to submit to Him, however anxious they are to do still more mischief to the sons of men. Yes, Jesus reigns from the bottomless gulf to the heights of heaven. Far off, where the sun now gilds the Western hills, and yonder, in the East where we shall watch for His return, over all those regions Jesus reigns. Let His people proclaim it without fear, "The Lord is King." The fact that He is now reigning cheers our hearts.

> *Rejoice, the Lord is King,*
> *Your Lord and King adore;*
> *Mortals, give thanks and sing,*
> *And triumph evermore:*
> *Lift up the heart, lift up the voice,*
> *Rejoice aloud, ye saints, rejoice.*

The Necessity for Christ's Reign

It is not merely that He shall, He can, or He may, but He *"must* reign."* Let us see why He must.

The first argument is the weakest of all, yet one that has much force in it: *all His servants say that He shall reign.* Weak as the twelve apostles were and the immediate followers of Christ, they said that He must reign, and they meant it, and they lived to make it true, and almost all the nations on the earth heard of Jesus within a century after He had been taken up to heaven. Then came the kings of the earth and set themselves against Him, and they said that He should not reign, but the martyrs came and yielded up their lives with joy, each one singing "He must reign." While the amphitheaters ran with blood, other champions came into the ring, each one uttering the watchword: "He must reign." The persecuted saints of God were mocked by the kings of the earth; each individual believer was weak, but they came by tens, by hundreds, by thousands, till the kings threw away their swords and quenched their thirst in sheer despair, and they agreed that, nominally at least, Christ should reign, for His disciples would have it so.

And now, today, it becomes us not to speak vauntingly, but if persecuting times should ever come again, many of those who say the least about it would be among the first to go boldly to be burned at the stake or to submit their bodies to torture for the love of the Lord Jesus Christ. There are thousands of Christians now who only need the dire necessity again to rise, and they would come forward with cheerfulness to yield their lives for their Lord, declaring that "He must reign," whatever might become of them. We must never let His standard fall or even tremble in the day of battle. Forward, you sons of heroes, in the name of Him who bled and died for you! Never let there be any question in your mind whether "He must reign" or not. The sun may cease to shine, and the moon forget her nightly marches, but Jesus must reign. It must be so, for His people declare it.

I said, however, that this was the weakest of reasons, and there are many far stronger ones. "He must reign," for *He is Jehovah's Heir*—the "heir of all things" (Heb. 1:2). Kings cannot always ensure the putting of their crowns upon the heads of their sons. When they die, perhaps a rebellion breaks out and overthrows the dynasty, but what power can overturn the divine dynasty and rob the Heir of God of His dominions?

"He must reign," for *by nature He is a King*. He was born a King; you might have seen something of sovereignty in His eyes when He first opened them upon earth's light. The wise men from the East brought gifts that showed that they recognized the royalty of the newborn babe of Bethlehem. Every characteristic of the life of Christ is royal. Jesus is no tyrant king. He is the people's King, but a true King in every part of His being. There is nothing mean or low or selfish about Him. Every motion of His hand is princely as He feeds the multitudes or heals their sicknesses, and every glance of His eye is kingly as He weeps over man's sin and fall or as He rebukes man's transgression.

"He must reign," *for He deserves that honor*. You cannot see Him voluntarily yielding up His soul to death so that He might redeem His people by His blood, and you cannot hear His cry "My God, my God, why has thou forsaken me?" without feeling that if there is justice in the courts of heaven, the death of Christ upon the cross cannot be the end of Him. The terrible shame must be rewarded, and how can it be rewarded except by the brightest crown that can possibly be imagined or by something brighter even than that? Reign He must, for He was so good, so generous, so self-sacrificing, so oblivious of Himself in death. We should lose our faith in deity if we could lose faith in the reign of Christ as the reward of all that He suffered upon the cross.

Besides, "He must reign," *for who is to stop Him?* In the olden days, many tried to do so, but He defeated them all. The prince of darkness came to Him in the wilderness and offered Him a paltry trinket in the place of His true crown, but the tempter was repulsed by the sentence, "It is written" (Matt. 4:4). The prince of darkness came again and again but found nothing in Christ upon which he could lay his hand, and before long, Christ will have the great adversary beneath His foot and finally bruise his head. All the evil forces upon the face of the earth cannot stand against Christ, for if upon the accursed tree He defeated them in His weakness, He will surely conquer them in the time of His strength. He trod them under His foot when He died. How much more completely shall He vanquish them now that He is risen! He scattered them like chaff before the wind with His dying breath. How much more shall He do it now in the fullness of His resurrection life! Rejoice, O Christians, in the fact that there is nothing that can stand against Jesus!

"He must reign" for the best of all reasons—*the Father has decreed it.* "Yet have I set my king upon my holy hill of Zion" (Ps. 2:6). God wills it, and that stands for us as a sufficient reason, and God is working it. Omnipotence is on the side of Christ. We see Him not yet at the head of His heavenly armies, but He is there, and He is even now going forth conquering and to conquer, and everything that happens is working out the decree that Christ must be King of kings and Lord of lords.

There Is a Progress About His Kingdom

His kingdom is growing; it becomes more and more visible among the sons of men. I am not going into prophecies; I leave them for wiser persons than I am. I am more at home in Matthew, Mark, Luke, and John than in the deeps of Revelation. But this one thing I do know from the Word of the Lord, that, first of all, *"He must reign" lovingly over all His elect.* Some of them are hard to bring in, but they must come sooner or later. Christ Himself said, "And other sheep I have, which are not of this fold: them also I must bring" (John 10:16). Some of them are with us now; they have long resisted mercy's call, but they will have to yield. The Lord says, "Compel them to come in" (Luke 14:23), and come in they must, for "He must reign." He will not suffer one of the sheep He bought with His blood to be lost on the mountains or one single soul that He ransomed from the enemy to abide forever in captivity. "He must reign" over them, and He will; and the day shall come when He shall pass all His sheep, one by one, under the hand of Him who counts them, and they will all be there, and the tale of the flock shall be complete; not one shall be devoured by the wolf. The Shepherd shall say to His Father in that day, "Those that thou gavest me I have kept, and none of them is lost" (John 17:12).

It also seems to me to be clear from the Scriptures that *in future ages Jesus Christ will reign over all nations.* I do not believe that the great drama of the world's history will end till truth is triumphant. I read concerning the Messiah, "He shall have dominion also from sea to sea, and from the river unto the ends of the earth. They that dwell in the wilderness shall bow before him; and his enemies shall lick the dust" (Ps. 72:8–9). The North shall give up, and the South shall no longer keep back, but they shall bring His sons from afar and His daughters from the ends of the earth. I cannot help expecting a period when "the glory of the LORD shall be revealed, and all flesh shall see it together: for the mouth of the LORD hath spoken it" (Isa. 40:5). Happy day! Oh, that it might soon arrive! Push on with mercy's work, O missionaries and evangelists! Toil on, preachers and teachers, for "He must reign." Ours is not a losing cause; Jesus must yet subdue the nations and be acknowledged by them as Lord and God.

I know also that He must *one day reign over all mankind*, whether by their willing consent or in spite of their opposition, for to Him every knee shall bow and every tongue shall "confess that Jesus Christ is Lord, to the glory of God the Father" (Phil. 2:11).

And over and above that, I look for a time when *Jesus Christ will reign upon this earth over all nature*, when, all His enemies being subdued, the new Jerusalem shall come down out of heaven upon the earth, prepared as a bride adorned for her husband. Read the Revelation, and you will find that much that we generally apply to heaven is really a description of what is to take place upon this earth. I hope it is not mere poetic fancy that leads me to believe that the mists that now swathe this planet and make her dim in comparison with her sister stars will one day all be swept away, and she shall shine out as bright as in the pristine morning when the sons of God shouted for joy at the sight of the new creation (Job 38:7). I think it is no fiction to believe that the day shall come when a restored manhood, in connection with the personal reign of Christ, shall have dominion over all the fowl of the air and the fish of the sea, and when it shall not be a metaphor but a realized fact that "the leopard shall lie down with the kid; and the calf and the young lion and the fatling together; and a little child shall lead them" (Isa. 11:6), when whispers of blasphemy shall not merely be drowned in thunders of adoration but shall not even be known, when the last taint and trace of sin shall have disappeared and the earth shall shine as if she had never been defiled and the days of her mourning shall be forever ended. And "Glory, glory, glory" shall be the song from sunrise to sunset, and the night watches shall be kept with music of praise, and angels shall go to and fro between the throne above and the throne below, and the new heavens and the new earth shall be seen, wherein dwells righteousness.

Then comes the grand climax, when He shall "put all enemies under his feet"—not annihilate them, not exterminate them, not convert them, but put them under His feet. There shall still be a devil, but he shall be a devil under Christ's feet. Lost spirits there shall still be, but the great Conqueror shall hold them down beneath His almighty heel. Death shall be destroyed. "The last enemy that shall be destroyed is death" (1 Cor. 15:26). We shall remember that men died; we shall ourselves remember that we passed beneath the power of death, but all the bitterness of death will be past so far as we are concerned. Through Christ's death, eternal life has become ours. Oh, what a prospect opens up before me! Let your faith project itself into the glorious future of which I have been reminding you. It may be much nearer than you have imagined. If you listen intently, you may hear the chariot wheels of the coming King. Be ready to greet Him whenever He comes. It may be tonight as the clock sounds midnight. Will you be ready to hail Him joyfully as your long-expected King?

How do I stand in relation to the great event thus predestined? What is my connection with the triumph of Christ? Am I one of His friends or one of His enemies? Do you yield that He is reigning over you? Shall He be King over you? If you want to have Him in any other terms than these, you cannot have Him at all, for "He must reign." Either you must let Him reign over you, or you will have to lie beneath His feet. Have you ever reckoned what will be the weight of the rejected love of God incarnate, who died for sinners and yet is rejected by myriads despite His unspeakable love? Take your pen and calculate that weight if you can: omnipotence indignant that eternal love was slighted, omniscience aroused to anger by the fact that divine compassion such as could never have been dreamed of was tramped under foot by impudent sons of men. In the name of the God who made the heavens and the earth and who made each of us, I entreat you to yield to that Christ who is your rightful King. Bow before Him now, yield yourself to Him, and trust Him. He will come with the sound of trumpet and with angel guards attending Him, swift to judge and stern to punish. Prepare to meet your King!

*P*ause, then, and let your soul's eye behold again this view of things. God has reigned from the first day; God shall reign when days are gone. Everywhere He is the reigning God—reigning when Pharaoh said, "Who is the LORD, that I should obey his voice?" (Exod. 5:2), as much as when Miriam took her timbrel and said, "Sing ye to the LORD, for he hath triumphed gloriously" (Exod. 15:21). Reigning when scribe and Pharisee, Jew and Roman, nailed the Only-begotten Son to the cross as much as when the angelic cohorts shouted in triumph, "Lift up your heads, O ye gates; and be ye lifted up, ye everlasting doors; and the King of glory shall come in" (Ps. 24:7). He reigns amid all the calamities that sweep the globe as much as He shall reign in the millennial days of peace ahead. Jehovah is always King and shall be King forever and ever. O blessed children, who have such a King for your father, for this unconquerable King sits securely on His throne. In the person of His dear Son He walks among our golden candlesticks and holds our stars in His right hand.

Chapter Nine

The Unconquerable King

And at the end of the days I Nebuchadnezzar lifted up mine eyes unto heaven, and mine understanding returned unto me, and I blessed the most High, and I praised and honoured him that liveth for ever, whose dominion is an everlasting dominion, and his kingdom is from generation to generation: And all the inhabitants of the earth are reputed as nothing: and he doeth according to his will in the army of heaven, and among the inhabitants of the earth: and none can stay his hand, or say unto him, What doest thou?—Daniel 4:34–35.

No one has ever numbered Nebuchadnezzar with the prophets or believed his language to be inspired. We have before us simply a declaration made by an uninspired man after passing through a most extraordinary experience. He had been among the greatest and proudest of men; he suddenly fell into the condition of a grass-eating ox by losing his reason; and upon being restored, he acknowledged publicly the hand of the Most High. I take from his language a most accurate statement of sublime doctrine that is clearly stated by the Holy Spirit in different parts of Scripture. It is a singular instance of how, when God comes to deal with men in afflicting providences, He can make them clearly see many great truths concerning Himself and can constrain them to express their conviction in identically the same way as they would have done if His own Spirit had dictated the terms. There are certain parts of the divine character that even the unspiritual cannot avoid seeing; and after passing through certain processes of suffering humiliation, the man is compelled to add his witness to the testimony of God's Spirit with regard to the divine character. Every single word that Nebuchadnezzar utters here can be backed up and supported by undoubtedly inspired words of men sent of God to proclaim infallible truth.

The Doctrinal Instruction

Nebuchadnezzar plainly states the doctrine of *the eternal self-existence of God*. "I blessed the most High, and I praised and honoured him that liveth for ever." If this word needed to be confirmed, we would refer you to the language of John in Revelation 4:9–10, where we find him describing the living creatures and the twenty-four elders as giving glory and honor and thanks "to him that sat on the throne, who liveth for ever and ever." Better still, listen to the witness of our Redeemer, "the Father hath life in himself" (John 5:26). Space does not allow the host of confirmative passages, for the eternal self-existence of God is taught throughout the Scriptures and is implied in the name that belongs only to the true God, Jehovah, "I AM THAT I AM" (Exod. 3:14). Note that it was not "I was" or "I will be," but it is "I AM," the only being, the root of existence, the immutable and eternal One. He also could say, "I am God, and there is none else" (Isa. 45:22). He declares, "I lift up my hand to heaven, and say, I live for ever" (Deut. 32:40). He is the only one underived, self-existent, self-sustained Being. Let us know that the Lord God whom we worship is the only being who necessarily and from His own nature exists. No other being could have been but for His sovereign will, nor could it continue were that will suspended. He is the only light of life, all others are reflections of His beams. There must be God, but there was no such necessity that there should be any other intelligences. In all the future, God must be, but the necessity for the continuance of other spirits lies in His will and not in the very nature of things. The immortality of spirits implied in passages such as Matthew 25:46, "these shall go away into everlasting punishment: but the righteous into life eternal," is the result of His own resolve to make spirits whose duration should be eternal; and though He will never withdraw the endowment of immortality that He has bestowed, yet the reason for eternal existence is not in the beings but entirely in Himself, for essentially "[He] only hath immortality" (1 Tim. 6:16). All that is created, if it had so pleased God to ordain, might have been as transient as a sunbeam and vanished as speedily as the rainbow from the cloud.

God is independent—the only being who is so. We must find food with which to repair the daily wastes of the body; we are dependent upon light and heat and innumerable external agencies, and we are above all and primarily dependent upon the outgoings of the divine power toward us. But the I AM is self-sufficient and all-sufficient. He was as glorious before He made the world as He is now; He was as great, as blessed, as divine in all His attributes before sun and moon and stars leaped into existence as He is now; and if He should blot all out as man erases the writing from his pencil or as the potter breaks the vessel he has made, He would be nonetheless the supreme and ever-blessed God. Nothing of God's being is derived from another, but all that exists is derived from Him. The hills and mountains, seas and stars, men and angels, heavens and heaven of heavens minister nothing to Him who made them, but they all stand together in existence flowing from the Creator.

God ever lives in this respect, that He undergoes no sort of change; all His creatures must from their constitution undergo more or less of a mutation. Of them all it is decreed: "They shall perish, but thou shalt endure: yea, all of them shall wax old like a garment; as a vesture shalt thou change them, and they shall be changed: but thou art the same, and thy years shall have no end" (Ps. 102:26–27). Our life is made of changes. From childhood we hasten to youth, from youth we leap to adulthood, from adulthood we fade into old age; our changes are as many as our days. Lighter than a feather, more frail than the flower of the field, brittle as glass, fleeting as a meteor, tossed to and fro and quenched as a spark, Lord, "What is man?" (Ps. 8:4). There comes to us all in the time appointed the great and ultimate change in which the spirit is separated from the body, to be followed by another in which the divided manhood shall be reunited; but with God there are no changes of this or any other kind. Has He not declared, "I am the LORD, I change not" (Mal. 3:6)? God is essentially and evermore pure Spirit and consequently undergoes no variableness or shadow of a turning. Of none of the creatures can this be said. Immutability is an attribute of God only. The things created were once new, they are growing old, and they will become older still; but the Lord has no time, He dwells in eternity. There is no moment of beginning with the Eternal, no starting point from which to calculate age. From of old He was the Ancient of Days: "from everlasting to everlasting, thou art God" (Ps. 90:2). Let your mind retreat as far as its capacities will allow into the remote past of old eternity, and there it finds Jehovah alone in the fullness of His glory. Then let the same thought flash forward into the far-off future, as far as unreined imagination can bear it, and there it behold the Eternal, unchanged, unchangeable. He works changes and effects changes, but He Himself abides the same.

That He lives forever is the result, not only of His essential and necessary self-existence, of His independence, and of His unchangeableness but also of the fact that there is no conceivable force that can ever wound, injure, or destroy Him. If we were profane enough to imagine the Lord to be vulnerable, where is the bow and arrow that could reach Him on His throne? What javelin shall pierce Jehovah's buckler? Let all the nations of the earth arise and rage against God, how shall they reach His throne? They cannot even shake His footstool. If all the angels should rebel against the Great King and their squadrons should advance in serried ranks to besiege the palace of the Most High, He has but to will it and they would wither as autumn leaves. Reserved in chains of darkness, the opponents of His power would forever become mementos of His wrath. None can touch Him; He is the God who ever lives. Let us who delight in the living God bow down before Him and humbly worship Him as the God in whom we live and move and have our being.

In our text we next find Nebuchadnezzar asserting *the everlasting dominion of God*. He said, "[God's] dominion is an everlasting dominion, and his kingdom is from generation to generation." The God whom we serve not only exists but also reigns. No other position would be fitting for Him but that of unlimited sovereignty over all His creatures. "The LORD hath prepared his throne in the heavens; and his kingdom ruleth over all" (Ps. 103:19). As David said, so also say we, "Thine, O LORD, is the greatness, and the power, and the glory, and the victory, and the majesty: for all that is in the heaven and in the earth is thine; thine is the kingdom, O LORD, and thou art exalted as head above all" (1 Chron. 29:11). "The LORD sitteth upon the flood; yea, the LORD sitteth King for ever" (Ps. 29:10).

The Lord is naturally the ruler of all, but who shall pretend to rule over Him? He is not to be judged of man's finite reason, for He does great things that we cannot comprehend. Amazing is the impertinence of man, when the creature dares to sit in judgment on the Creator. His character is not to be called into question; only the boundless arrogance of our pride would so dare to insult the holy God. "Be still, and know that I am God" (Ps. 46:10) is a sufficient reply to such madness. The Lord's place is on the throne, and our place is to obey; it is His to govern, ours to serve; His to do as He wills, and ours to make that will our constant delight.

Remember, then, that in the universe God is actually reigning. Never let us conceive of God as being infinitely great but not exerting His greatness, infinitely able to reign but as yet a mere spectator of events. It is not so. The Lord reigns even now. Though in one sense we pray, "Thy kingdom come" (Matt. 6:10), yet in another we say, "For thine is the kingdom, and the power, and the glory, for ever" (vs. 13). God does not hold a bare title to kingship, but He is actually King. The government is upon His shoulders, the reins of management are in His hands. Even at this hour He speaks to the sons of men, "See now that I, even I, am he, and there is no god with me: I kill, and I make alive; I wound, and I heal: neither is there any that can deliver out of my hand" (Deut. 32:39). He "hath scattered the proud in the imagination of their hearts. He hath put down the mighty from their seats, and exalted them of low degree" (Luke 1:51–52). Events appear to fly at random like the dust in the whirlwind, but it is not so. The rule of the Omnipotent extends over all thing at all times. Nothing is left to its own chance happening, but in wisdom all things are governed. Glory be to the omnipresent and invisible Lord of all.

This divine kingdom appeared very plainly to the once proud Nebuchadnezzar, king of Babylon, to be an everlasting one. The reign of the ever-living God extends as other kingdoms cannot, "from generation to generation." The mightiest king inherits power and soon yields his scepter to his successor; the Lord has no beginning of days nor end of years; predecessor and successor are words inapplicable to Him. There is no greater power than God; there is no other power but that which proceeds from God, for "God hath spoken once; twice have I heard this; that power belongeth unto God" (Ps. 62:11). Hence, His monarch cannot be subdued and must be everlasting.

Dynasties on earth pass away, but God the ever-living asks none to succeed Him. Internal corruptions have often blasted empires that stood aloft like forest trees, defiant of the storm. At the core, the tree was rotten, and before long, weakened by decay, it tottered to its fall; but the infinitely holy God has no injustice, error, partiality, or evil motive in the government of His affairs. Everything is arranged with spotless holiness, unimpeachable justice, unvarying fidelity, untarnished truth, amazing mercy, and overflowing love. All the elements of His kingdom are most conservative, because radically right. There is no evil leaven in the council chamber of omniscience, no corruption on the judgment seat of heaven; hence "God sitteth upon the throne of his holiness" (Ps. 47:8). Because His throne is holy, we rejoice that it can never be moved.

Pause, then, and let your soul's eye behold again this view of things. God has reigned from the first day; God shall reign when days are gone. Everywhere He is the reigning God—reigning when Pharaoh said, "Who is the LORD, that I should obey his voice?" (Exod. 5:2), as much as when Miriam took her timbrel and said, "Sing ye to the LORD, for he hath triumphed gloriously" (Exod. 15:21). Reigning when scribe and Pharisee, Jew and Roman, nailed the Only-begotten Son to the cross as much as when the angelic cohorts shouted in triumph, "Lift up your heads, O ye gates; and be ye lifted up, ye everlasting doors; and the King of glory shall come in" (Ps. 24:7). He reigns amid all the calamities that sweep the globe as much as He shall reign in the millennial days of peace ahead. Jehovah is always King and shall be King forever and ever. O blessed children, who have such a King for your father, for this unconquerable King sits securely on His throne. In the person of His dear Son He walks among our golden candlesticks and holds our stars in His right hand.

Nebuchadnezzar, humbled before God, uses, in the third place, extraordinary language with regard to *the nothingness of mankind*. "All the inhabitants of the earth are reputed as nothing." This is Nebuchadnezzar, but his words are confirmed by Isaiah: "Behold, the nations are as a drop of a bucket" (Isa. 40:15), the unnoticed drop that remains in the bucket after it has been emptied, a thing too inconsiderable to be worthy of notice. Isaiah adds, "And are counted as the small dust of the balance: behold, he taketh up the isles as a very little thing," as the dust that falls upon scales but is not sufficient to affect the balance in any degree whatever. If Nebuchadnezzar goes far, Isaiah, inspired by the Spirit, goes farther; the one calls the nations "nothing," and the other "less than nothing and vanity." Gather up all the nations together in one mighty congregation, and yet all of them are as nothing.

Generations pass like the successive series of forest leaves; so do the nations. They are all nothing in comparison with God. He stands for all in all and comprehends all, and all the rest are but so many valueless cinders till His unit makes them of account. Let me remind you that every person who is spiritually taught of God is made to feel experientially on his own account his own utter nothingness. When his inner eye, like that of Job, beholds the Lord, he abhors himself, he shrinks into the earth, he feels he cannot contrast or compare himself with the Most High even for a second. We discover we are nothing in our election: "Ye have not chosen me, but I have chosen you" (John 15:16). We were nothing in our redemption; we contributed nothing to that price that Jesus paid: "I have trodden the winepress alone; and of the people there was none with me" (Isa. 63:3). We are nothing in our regeneration: can the spiritually dead help the blessed God to quicken them? "It is the spirit that quickeneth; the flesh profiteth nothing" (John 6:63). We shall, when we get to heaven, make it part of our adoration to confess that we are less than nothing and vanity but that God is all in all. Therefore, shall we cast our crowns at His feet and give Him all the praise forever and ever.

We turn now to the next sentence, which reveals *the divine power at work sovereignly.* "He doeth according to his will in the army of heaven, and among the inhabitants of the earth." This is easy to understand in reference to the celestial host, for we know that God's will is done in heaven: we devoutly pray that it may yet be done on earth after the same fashion. The angels find it their heaven to be obedient to the God of heaven. Under the term "army of heaven" is comprehended fallen angels who were once numbered with that band but were expelled from heaven for their rebellion. Devils unwillingly, but yet of necessity, fulfill the will of God. "Whatsoever the LORD pleased, that did he in heaven, and in earth, in the seas, and all deep places" (Ps. 135:6). When we read in the text that on earth God's will is done, we see that it is so in a measure among the righteous whose renewed hearts seek after God's glory; but the truth goes further, for that will is also accomplished in the unrighteous and by those who know Him not, even in those whose will is determined to oppose Him. Still, in some way unknown to us, the will of God is achieved (Prov. 19:21; Acts 4:27–28). The miracle of divine glory lies in that He has made men free agents, has endowed them with a will, with which He will never interfere except according to the laws of mind, and leaves them absolutely free to do what they will and they will universally of themselves to do contrary to His will. And yet, such is the magnificent strategy of heaven, such is the marvelous force of the divine mind, that despite everything, the will of God is done.

Can you understand it, for I cannot, how man is a free agent, a responsible agent, so that his sin is his own willful sin and lies with him and never with God, and yet at the same time God's purposes are fulfilled and His will is done even by demons and corrupt people? I cannot comprehend it: without hesitation I believe it, and rejoice to do so, but I never hope to comprehend it. I worship a God I never expect to comprehend. If I could grasp Him in the hollow of my hand, I could not call Him my God; and if I could understand His dealings so that I could read them as a child reads his spelling book, I could not worship Him. But because He is so infinitely great, I find truth here, truth there, truth multiform; and if I cannot compress it into one system, I know it is all clear to Him, and I am content that He should know what I know not. It is mine today to adore and obey, and when He sees fit, I shall know more and adore better.

It is my firm belief that everything in heaven and earth and hell will be seen to be, in the long run, parts of the divine plan, yet never is God the author or the accomplice of sin, never is He otherwise than the hater of sin and the avenger of unrighteousness. Sin rests with man, wholly with man, and yet by some strange overruling force, Godlike and mysterious, God's supreme will is accomplished. Nothing, including sin, is left outside the control of providence, and therefore are we comforted.

Let us now consider the fifth part of the text: "None can stay his hand, or say unto him, What doest thou?" I gather from this that *God's design is irresistible and unimpeachable.* We are told by some annotators that the original has in it an allusion to a blow given to a child's hand to make the child cease from some forbidden action. None can treat the Lord in that manner. None can hinder Him or cause Him to pause. He has might to do what He wills. So also says Isaiah: "Woe unto him that striveth with his Maker! Let the potsherd strive with the potsherds of the earth. Shall the clay say to him that fashioneth it, What makest thou? or thy work, He hath no hands?" (Isa. 45:9). Man is powerless to resist the design of God. Usually he does not know God's design, although he blunderingly thinks he does. Often in opposing that apparent design, he fulfills the secret design of God against his will. If man did set himself with all his might against the will of God, yet as the chaff cannot resist the wind, as it is not possible for the wax to resist the fire, neither can man effectually resist the absolute will and sovereign good pleasure of the Most High. Only here is our comfort; it is right that God should have this might, because He always uses His might with strictest rectitude. God cannot will to do anything unjust, ungenerous, unkind, ungodlike. God is love. God is holy. God is the law. God is love, and doing as He wills, He wills to love. God is holy, and doing as He wills, He wills holiness. God is the law, and doing as He wills, He wills justice, He wills truth. "Shall not the Judge of all the earth do right?" (Gen. 18:25). Act then this day as you would do in such a case, for you are truly in His hands.

Practical Instruction

I think the first lesson is, *how wise it is to be at one with Him*! I am bowed before the majesty in this text. I felt within my soul, "How I long to be perfectly at one with this infinitely mighty, glorious, and holy God. How can I dare to be His enemy?" I felt then if I had not yielded before, I must yield now, subdued before Him. He invites us to come. He might have commended you to depart. In His infinite sovereignty He has appointed Christ Jesus to be the Savior of all men. Come and accept that Savior by faith.

How encouraging this is to those who are at one with God! If He is on our side, who shall be against us? "The LORD of hosts is with us; the God of Jacob is our refuge" (Ps. 46:7). Be glad that you have One to trust in to whom nothing is impossible, who can and will achieve His purposes. "The LORD reigneth; let the earth rejoice; let the multitude of isles be glad thereof" (Ps. 97:1).

How joyful this thought should be *to all holy workers*! You and I have enlisted on the side of God and of His Christ, and though the powers against us seem very strong, yet the invisible King will surely put them to the rout before long. The greatest problems of this world, when the Lord Jesus smites them with the rod of iron, see how the pieces fly! This He shall do before long. He will lift the might of His terrible arm and bring down His iron rod; then shall it be seen that the truth as it is in Jesus must and shall prevail.

How this should *help you who suffer*! If God does it all, and nothing happens apart from God, even the wickedness and cruelty of man still being overruled by Him, you readily may submit. How graciously and with what good face can you kiss the hand that smites you! The husband has been taken to heaven; the property has melted; God has permitted it. You were robbed, you say; well, think not so much of the second cause, but look to the great first cause. It is your God who is in it all, your Father God, the infinitely good.

Which would you desire to have done on earth, your will or God's will? If you are wise, you want His will. Then accept the ways of providence. Since God appoints them, accept them with grateful praise. Herein is true sacrifice to God when we can say, "Though he slay me, yet will I trust in him" (Job 13:15). We have received good at His hands, and we have blessed Him. Unbelievers might have done the same, but if we receive evil and still bless Him, this is grace, this is the work of His Holy Spirit. If we can bow before His crushing strokes and feel that if the crushing of us by the weight of His hand will bring Him honor, we are content; this is true faith. Give us grace enough, O Lord, to be Your faithful servants even to suffering's bitterest end. Oh, to have the mind thus subjected to God! Some kick at the doctrine of divine sovereignty, but I fear it is because they have a rebellious, unhumbled spirit. Those who feel obedient to God cannot yield Him too absolute an authority. Only a rebellious child in a house wishes the father to be tied by rules and regulations. No, my Father must do right; let Him do what He wills.

The Right Spirit

The first is *humble adoration*. We do not worship enough. Even in our public gatherings we do not have enough worship. Oh, worship the King! Bow your head—bow your spirit rather—and adore Him who lives forever and ever. Your thoughts, your emotions, these are better than sacrifices to be offered on the altar: God will accept them. Worship Him with lowliest reverence, for you are nothing, and He is all in all.

Next let the spirit of your heart be that of *unquestioning acquiescence*. He wills it! I will do it, or I will bear it. God help you to live in perfect resignation.

Next to that, exercise the spirit of *reverent love*. Do I tremble before God? Then I must seek more grace that I may love Him as He is, not love Him when my thoughts have diminished Him of His splendor or robbed Him of His glory, but love Him even as an absolute sovereign, for I see that sovereignty exercised through Jesus Christ, my shield and His Anointed. Let me love my God and King and be a courtier, happy to be admitted near His throne, to behold the light of the Infinite Majesty.

Finally, let our spirit be that of *profound delight*. I believe there is no doctrine to the mature believer that contains such a deep sea of delight as this. The Lord reigns! The Lord is King forever and ever! Then all is well. When you get away from God, you get away from peace. When the soul dives into Him and feels that all is in Him, she feels a calm delight, a peace like a river, a joy unspeakable. Strive after that delight, and then go and express it in your songs of praise. Lift up your hearts in His praise, for whoever "offereth praise glorifieth [God]" (Ps. 50:23).

May the Lord bring us, through faith in Jesus Christ, into harmony with this ever-blessed and ever-living God, and unto Him be praise and glory forever and ever.

Most readers consider these words to mean salvation from hell. They are partially correct, but the notion is highly defective. It is true that Christ does save men from the penalty of their guilt; He does take those to heaven who deserve the eternal wrath and displeasure of the Most High; it is true that He does blot out iniquity, transgression, and sin and that the iniquities of the remnant of His people are passed over for the sake of His blood and atonement. But that is not the whole meaning of the words to save. This deficient explanation lies at the root of mistakes that many theologians have made and by which they have surrounded their system of divinity with mist. While it means to pluck men as brands from the burning, it means infinitely more than this. By the words to save, I understand the whole of the great work of salvation, from the first holy desire, the first spiritual conviction, onward to complete sanctification, all this done of God through Jesus Christ. Christ is not only mighty to carry those to heaven who repent and believe but also mighty to give men new hearts and to work faith in them; He is mighty not merely to give heaven to one who desires it but also to make the man who hates holiness to love it, to constrain the despiser of His name to bend his knee before Him, and to make the most abandoned reprobate turn from the error of his ways.

Chapter Ten

A Mighty Savior

Mighty to save—Isaiah 63:1.

ISAIAH, OF COURSE, IS REFERRING to our blessed Lord Jesus Christ, who is described as coming "from Edom, with dyed garments from Bozrah," and who, when it is questioned who He is, replies, "I that speak in righteousness, mighty to save." It would be appropriate, then, to make a few statements concerning the mysteriously complex person of the man and God whom we call our Redeemer, Jesus Christ our Savior. It is one of the mysteries of Christianity that we are taught to believe that Christ is God and yet a man. According to Scripture, we hold that He is "very *God*" (1 Thess. 5:23), equal and co-eternal with the Father, possessing, as His Father does, all divine attributes in an infinite degree. He participated with His Father in all the acts of His divine might; He was concerned in the decree of election, in the fashioning of the covenant, in the creation of the angels, in the making of the world when it was wheeled from nothing into space, and in the ordering of this fair frame of nature. Before any of these acts, the divine Redeemer was the eternal Son of God. "From everlasting to everlasting, thou art God" (Ps. 90:2).

Nor did He cease to be God when He became man. Paul tells us that He was equally the One "who is over all, God blessed for ever" (Rom. 9:5), when He was "a man of sorrows, and acquainted with grief" (Isa. 53:3), as before His incarnation. We have abundant proof of that in the constant affirmations of Scripture and, indeed, also in the miracles that He wrought. The raising of the dead, the walking on the water, the hushing of the winds, and the rending of the rocks—all those marvelous acts of His were strong and potent proofs that He was God, most truly God, even when He condescended to be man. And Scripture most certainly teaches us that He is God now, that He shares the throne of His Father—that He sits "far above all principality, and power, and might, and dominion, and every name that is named" (Eph. 1:21) and is the true and proper object of the worship and praise of all worlds.

We are equally taught to believe that He was *man*. Scripture informs us that on a day appointed, He came from heaven and did become man as well as God, taking upon Himself the nature of a babe in the manger of Bethlehem. From that babe, we are told that He grew to the stature of manhood and became like us in every respect except our sin. His sufferings, His hunger, and, above all, His death and burial are strong proofs that He was man, most truly man, while still being most truly God. We are told "a child is born, unto us a son is given," and yet, at the same time, He is the "Wonderful, Counselor, The mighty God, The everlasting Father, The Prince of Peace" (Isa. 9:6). Whoever would have a clear and right view of Jesus must not mingle His natures. We must consider Him not as a God diluted into deified manhood or as a mere man officially exalted to the Godhead but as being two distinct natures in one person; not God melted in man nor man made into God, but man and God taken into union together. Therefore, do we trust in Him as the divine Mediator, Son of God and Son of Man. This is the person who is our Savior. It is this glorious yet mysterious being of whom the text speaks when it says that He is "mighty to save."

This is the might and majesty of the incarnate Son of God. You believe Him to be the Regent of providence, the King of death, the Conqueror of hell, the Lord of angels, the Master of storms, and the God of battles, and therefore you need no proof that He is mighty. But how is it that He is mighty to save?

Defining the Words *to Save*

Most readers consider these words to mean salvation from hell. They are partially correct, but the notion is highly defective. It is true that Christ does save men from the penalty of their guilt; He does take those to heaven who deserve the eternal wrath and displeasure of the Most High; it is true that He does blot out iniquity, transgression, and sin and that the iniquities of the remnant of His people are passed over for the sake of His blood and atonement. But that is not the whole meaning of the words *to save*. This deficient explanation lies at the root of mistakes that many theologians have made and by which they have surrounded their system of divinity with mist. While it means to pluck men as brands from the burning, it means infinitely more than this. By the words *to save*, I understand the whole of the great work of salvation, from the first holy desire, the first spiritual conviction, onward to complete sanctification, all this done of God through Jesus Christ. Christ is not only mighty to carry those to heaven who repent and believe but also mighty to give men new hearts and to work faith in them; He is mighty not merely to give heaven to one who desires it but also to make the man who hates holiness to love it, to constrain the despiser of His name to bend his knee before Him, and to make the most abandoned reprobate turn from the error of his ways.

Some men say that "to save" means that Christ came into the world to put all men into a salvable state—to make the salvation of men possible by their own exertion. Christ came to do no such thing! He came into the world to put men into a saved state, not to put them where they could save themselves. He came to do the work in them and for them, from the first to the last. I would give up preaching if I believed that Christ came only to put men into a state where they might save themselves, for I know a little of the wickedness of men's hearts, because I know something of my own. Knowing how much men despise the religion of Christ, what success would I have preaching a gospel that depended upon the voluntary response of an unrenewed heart?

If I did not believe that there was a power going forth with the word of Jesus that makes men willing in the day of His power and turns them from the error of their ways by the mighty, overwhelming, constraining force of a divine and mysterious influence, I should cease to glory in the cross of Christ. Christ is mighty to absolutely and entirely save men. This fact I regard as one of the grandest proofs of the divine character of the biblical revelation.

I have many times had doubts and fears, and where is the strong believer who has not sometimes wavered? I have said within myself, "Is this faith true that day after day I incessantly preach to the people? Is it true that this religion has an influence upon mankind?" I will tell you how I have reassured myself. I have looked upon hundreds and thousands around me who were once the vilest of the vile—drunkards, liars, foul-mouthed—and I now see them "clothed, and in [their] right mind" (Mark 5:15), walking in holiness and in the fear of God. I have said to myself, "This must be the truth because I see its marvelous effects. It is a power, an irresistible agent of good, that cannot be anything but truth."

I take it that the highest proof of Christ's power is not that He offers salvation, not that He offers you to take it if you like, but that when you reject it, when you hate it, when you despise it, He has the power to change your mind and make you think differently from your former thoughts, turning you from the error of your ways. This I believe to be the meaning of the text: "mighty to save."

But it is not all the meaning. Our Lord is mighty to make men repent, to quicken the dead in sin, to turn them from their sin. But He is exalted to do more than that: He is mighty to keep them Christians after He has made them so and mighty to preserve them in His fear and love until He consummates their spiritual existence in heaven. Christ's might does not lie in making a believer and then leaving him to take care of himself; but He who begins a good work in us carries it on; He who imparts the first spark of life in the dead soul gives afterward the life that prolongs the divine existence and bestows that mighty power that at last bursts asunder every bond of sin and lands the soul perfected in glory. We believe not only that Christ puts a man into a gracious state but also that He gives the man such an inward life and such a power within himself that he can no more turn back than the very sun in the heavens can cease to shine. "For it is God which worketh in you both to will and to do of his good pleasure" (Phil. 2:13). That is a Savior who is mighty to save.

Can We Prove That Christ Is Mighty to Save?

I will give you the strongest argument first, and I shall need only one. The argument is that He *has* done it. We need no other; it is superfluous to add another. He *has* saved men, in the full extent and meaning of the word that we have endeavored to explain.

Imagine the worst case possible. Think of the South Sea native who is a cannibal and glories in the scalps of the men he has murdered and the blood he has shed. That man bows before a block of wood and is a poor, debased, ignorant creature. Has Christ's gospel power to tame that man, to take the scalps from his side, to make him give up his bloody practices, renounce his gods, and become a Christian? We know that the gospel has this power because it has already done it through the work of missionaries who braved their lives to reach these natives. We have heard the story of the savage confronted by the love of the missionary, listening to the story of Jesus, then dropping his weapon and saying, "It is marvelous. The things that this man tells me are wonderful. I will sit and listen." He listens, and the tears roll down his cheeks; a feeling of humanity that never before burned within his soul is kindled in him. He says, "I believe in the Lord Jesus Christ," and soon the man is clothed and in his right mind and becomes in every respect a man—such a man as we could desire all men to be.

Now, we say, this is proof that Christ's gospel does not come to the mind that is prepared for it but prepares the mind for itself; that Christ does not merely put the seed into the ground that has been prepared beforehand but plows the ground and does all the work. He is so able to do all this. Ask our missionaries who are in Africa in the midst of some of the greatest barbarians in the world. Ask them whether Christ's gospel is mighty to save, and they will point to the village of the Hottentot and to the houses of the Kuraman, and they will say, "What has transformed these people but the word of the gospel of Jesus Christ?"

Proofs abound in heathen countries, but we also have proofs enough at home. I could tell you stories of some who have plunged headfirst into the blackest gulfs of sin, stories that would horrify you and me if we could allow them to recount their guilt. I could tell you how they have come into God's house with their teeth set against the minister, determined that they would not listen no matter what he might say, but it would be to scoff. They stayed a moment; some word arrested their attention; they thought within themselves, "I will hear that sentence." It was some terse, pointed saying that entered into their souls. They knew not how it happened, but they were spellbound and stood to listen a little longer; and eventually, unconsciously to themselves, the tears began to fall, and when they went away, they had a strange, mysterious feeling about them that led them to a private place. Down they fell on their knees; the story of their life was all told before God; He gave them peace through the blood of the Lamb, and they went to God's house, many of them to tell of the Savior who had found them.

Remember the case of John Newton, the great and mighty preacher of St. Mary, Woolnoth? He is an example of the power of God to change the heart as well as to give peace when the heart is changed. I often think within myself, "This is the greatest proof of the Savior's power." Let another doctrine be preached: will it do the same? If it will, why not let every man gather a crowd around him and preach it. Will it really do it? If it will, then the blood of men's souls must rest upon the man who does not boldly proclaim it. If he believes his gospel does save souls, how does he account for it that within an entire year there are no drunkards reclaimed or harlots made honest? Why? For this reason, that it is a poor dilution of Christianity. It is something like it, but it is not the bold, broad Christianity of the Bible; it is not the full gospel of the blessed God, for that *has* power to save. We say again that we have proof positive that Christ is mighty to save even the worst of men.

The best proof you can ever have of God's being mighty to save is that He saved *you.* Ah! It is a miracle if He should save the person who stands by your side, but it is more a miracle if He should save you. It is a miracle that He can take our deceitful hearts and by such a power cause us to love the gospel forever. "That which we have seen and heard declare we unto you" (1 John 1:3). When we have felt the change it works in our lives, then we speak of facts and not of imaginations, and we speak very boldly, "Jesus is mighty to save."

Why Christ Is Mighty to Save

First, if we understand salvation to mean the pardon of sin and salvation from hell, Christ is mighty to save *because of the infinite efficacy of His atoning blood.* Though we may be black with sin, Christ is able to make us whiter than the driven snow. You ask why. He is able to forgive because He has been punished for our sin. If you know yourself to be a sinner, if you have no hope or refuge before God but in Christ, then be it known that Christ is able to forgive, because He was once punished for the very sin that you have committed, and therefore He can freely remit because the punishment has been entirely paid by Him.

Once a poor Irishman came to me in my vestry. He announced himself something in this way: "Your reverence, I'm come to ask you a question." "In the first place," said I, "I am not a reverend, nor do I claim the title; and in the next place, why don't you go and ask your priest that question?" Said he, "Well, your rev—sir, I meant—I did go to him, but he did not answer me to my satisfaction exactly; so I have come to ask you, and if you will answer this you will set my mind at peace, for I am much disturbed about it." "What is the question?" I asked. "Why this. You say, and others say too, that God is able to forgive sin. Now, I can't see how He can be just and yet forgive sin: for I have been so greatly guilty that if God almighty does not punish me He *ought*. I feel that He would not be just if He were to suffer me to go without punishment. How, then, sir, can it be true that He can forgive and still retain the title of just?" "Well," said I, "it is through the blood and merits of Jesus Christ." "Ah!" said he, "but then I do not understand what you mean by that. It is the kind of answer I got from the priest, but I wanted him to explain it to me more fully."

"Well, then," I said, "I will tell you what I think to be the whole system of atonement, the essence of all the gospel. This is the way Christ is able to forgive. Suppose," said I, "you had killed someone. You were a murderer, you were condemned to die, and you deserved it." "Yes," said he, "I should deserve it." "Well, her Majesty is very desirous of saving your life, and yet at the same time universal justice demands that someone should die on account of the deed that is done. Now, how is she to manage it?" Said he, "That is the question. I cannot see how she can be inflexibly just and yet suffer me to escape." "Well," I said, "suppose I should go to her and say, 'Here is this poor Irishman, he deserves to be hanged, your Majesty. I cannot quarrel with the sentence, because it is just; but if you please, I so love him that if you were to hang me instead of him, I should be very willing.' If she agreed to it, what then? Would she be just in letting you go?" "Ay," said he, "I should think she would. Would she hang two for one thing? I should say not. I'd walk away, and there isn't a policeman who would touch me for it." "Ah!" said I, "that is how Jesus saves. 'Father,' He said, 'I love these poor sinners. Let me suffer instead of them!' 'Yes,' said the Father, 'you shall.' And on the tree He suffered and died for the punishment that all His elect people should have suffered, so that now all who believe on Him, thus proving themselves to be His chosen, may conclude that He was punished for them and that therefore they never be punished."

"Well," said he, looking me in the face once more, "I understand what you mean, but how is it, if Christ died for all men, that notwithstanding, some men are punished again? For that is unjust." "Ah!" said I, "I never told you that. I say to you that He has died for all who believe on Him and all who repent, and that He was punished for their sins so absolutely and so really that none of them shall ever be punished again." "Faith," said he, as he went down the stairs, "I am safe now. With all my sins I'll trust in the man who died for me, and so I shall be saved."

Yes, Christ is mighty to save, because God did not turn away the sword, but He sheathed it in His own Son's heart. He did not remit the debt, for it was paid in drops of precious blood; and now the great receipt is nailed to the cross, and our sins with it, so that we may go free if we are believers in Him.

In the wider sense of the words, understand "mighty to save" as meaning all that I have said it means. God does not save men by the eloquence of preachers or by the force of moral persuasion. He does it by the omnipotent influence of His divine Spirit. While men are hearing the Word, the Holy Spirit works repentance; He changes the heart and renews the soul. True, the preaching may be the instrument, but the Holy Spirit is the great agent. It is certain that the truth is the means of saving, but it is the Holy Spirit applying the truth that saves people. And with this power of the Holy Spirit we may go to the most degraded of men and never need fear but that God can save them. He is an Almighty Spirit, able to work wonders.

In the life of Whitefield, we read that sometimes under one of his sermons two thousand people would at once profess to be saved and were really saved. We ask why it was. At other times he preached just as powerfully and not one soul was saved. Why? Because in the one case the Holy Spirit went with the Word, and in the other case it did not. All the heavenly result of preaching is owing to the divine Spirit sent from above. I am nothing; it is God who does everything. "Who then is Paul, and who is Apollos, but ministers by whom ye believed, even as the Lord gave to every man?" (1 Cor. 3:5). It must be, "Not by might, nor by power, but by my spirit, saith the LORD of hosts" (Zech. 4:6).

Go forth, poor minister! You have no power to preach with polished diction and elegant refinement; go and preach as you can. The Spirit can make your feeble words more mighty than the most ravishing eloquence. Alas, for oratory! Alas, for eloquence! They have long been tried. We have had polished periods and finely turned sentences, but in what place have the people been saved by them? We have had grand language, but where have hearts been renewed? But now, "by the foolishness of preaching" (1 Cor. 1:21), by the simple utterance by a child of God's Word, He is pleased to save them that believe and turn sinners from the error of their ways.

Jesus as Mighty to Save

For ministers, let us learn to endeavor to preach in faith, nothing wavering. "O God," cries the minister as he falls to his knees. "I have preached and wept over my people. I have groaned for them, but they will not turn to you. Their hearts are like millstones. They will not weep for sin nor love the Savior." Then I think I see the angel standing at his elbow and whispering in his ear, "You are weak, but He is strong. You can do nothing, but He is mighty to save." It is not the instrument but the God. It is not the pen that the writer writes with that should receive the praise of his wisdom or the making of the volume, but it is the brain that thinks it and the hand that moves the pen. So in salvation. It is not the minister but the God who first designs the salvation and later uses the preacher to work it out. Preach on in faith, remembering that it is written, "So shall my word be that goeth forth out of my mouth: it shall not return unto me void, but it shall accomplish that which I please, and it shall prosper in the thing whereto I sent it" (Isa. 55:11).

Here also is encouragement for men and women who are praying to God for their friends. Mother, have you been groaning for your son for many years; he is now grown and left your house, but your prayers have not been heard. So you think, because you see no change in his life. Sometimes you think he will bring your gray hairs with sorrow to the grave. Perhaps you have said, "I will give him up and never pray for him again." Stop! By all that is holy and that is heavenly, stop! Utter not that resolution again; begin once more! You have prayed over him, wept over him, taught him in his youth, and you have often warned him since, but all to no avail. Do not give up your prayer, for remember that Christ is mighty to save. It may be that He waits to be gracious and has kept you waiting that you may know more of His graciousness when the mercy comes. But pray on. I have known mothers who prayed for their children for twenty years, and it was the mother's death that became the means for the saving of their children. Pray on, then, my sister; pray on, my brother! God shall yet bring your sons and daughters to His love and fear, and you shall rejoice over them in heaven, if you never do on earth.

Turn to Jesus, you who are weary. Come to Him because He bids you come. He is mighty to save. If you cannot pray, He can help you to do it. If you cannot repent, He can give you repentance. If you feel it is hard to believe, He can help you believe, for He is exalted on high to give repentance as well as to give remission of sins. Trust in Jesus; cast yourself on Him.

When death comes with all its terrors, it is usual for Satan to make a fierce inroad into the soul. Usually with many of the saints, if not in the last stage of death, yet some little time before it, there is a ferocious onslaught made by the great enemy of souls. And then he loves death, because death weakens the mind. The approach of death destroys some of the mental power and takes away from us for a season some of those spirits by which we have been cheered in better days. It makes us lie there, languid and faint and weary. Seeing his opportunity, the devil steals in upon us. Hence, I believe for this reason he is said to have the power of death, for I cannot believe that the devil has the power of death in any other sense but this, that it was originated by him and that he at such time generally displays the most of his malice and of his power. For it is certain that the devil has not the power of death so as to cause death. All the devils in hell could not take away the life of the smallest infant in the world, and though we lie gasping and sick so that the doctors despair of us, it is nothing but the design of the Almighty that can cause us to die, even in the extremity of our weakness. We rejoice to believe that an angel's arm cannot hurl us to the grave, even though it is the arm of that fallen archangel Lucifer. And we rejoice to know that afterward a myriad of angels cannot confine us there, so that neither for the locking of the door nor for the securing of it afterward does the devil have any power whatever over the Christian in death.

Chapter Eleven

The Destroyer Destroyed

That through death he might destroy him that had the power of death, that is, the devil—Hebrews 2:14.

IN GOD'S ORIGINAL PARADISE everything was happiness and joy and peace. If there is any evil, any suffering and pain, it is not God's work. God may permit it, overrule it, and out of it extract good, but the evil does not come from God. He Himself stands pure and perfect, the clean fountain out of which gushes forth sweet and pure waters. The devil's reign, on the contrary, contains nothing of good: "the devil sinneth from the beginning" (1 John 3:8), and his dominion has been one uniform course of temptation to evil and infliction of misery. Death is a part of Satan's dominion; he brought sin into the world when he tempted Eve to eat of the forbidden fruit, and with sin he brought also death into the world with all its train of woes. It is likely that there would have been no death if there had been no devil. If Satan had not tempted, perhaps man would not have revolted, and if man had not revolted, he would have lived forever without having to undergo the painful change that is caused by death.

I think death is the devil's masterpiece. With the solitary exception of hell, death is certainly the most satanic mischief that sin has accomplished. Nothing ever delighted the heart of the devil so much as when he found that the threatening would be fulfilled: "in the day that thou eatest thereof thou shalt surely die" (Gen. 2:17). Never was his malicious heart so full of hellish joy as when he saw Abel stretched upon the earth, slain by the club of his brother. "Aha!" said Satan. "This is the first of all intelligent creatures that has died. Oh, how I rejoice! This is the crowning hour of my dominion. It is true that I have marred the glory of this earth by my guileful temptation; it is true that the whole creation groans and travails in pain by reason of the evil that I have brought into it; but this, this is my masterpiece. I have killed man. I have brought death unto him, and here lies the first dead man."

Since that time, Satan has ever gloated over the death of the human race, and he has some cause for glory, for death has been universal. All have died. Though they had been wise as Solomon, their wisdom could not spare them; though they had been as virtuous as Moses, yet their virtue could not avert death. All have died, and therefore the devil has boasted in his triumph. But twice has he been defeated, and two have entered heaven without dying. However, the mass of mankind has had to feel the scythe of death; and the devil has rejoiced because this, his mightiest work, has had foundations broad as earth and a summit that reached as high as the virtues of mankind could climb.

There is something fearful in death. It is frightful even to him who has the most faith. It is only what we know comes after death—the heaven, the harp, the glory—that makes death bearable even to the believer. Death in itself must ever be an unutterably fearful thing to the sons of men. And oh, what ruin does it work! It darkens the windows of the eyes; it pulls down the polished pillars of the divine architecture of the body; it turns the inhabitant, the soul, out of its door and bids it fly to worlds unknown; and it leaves in place of a living man a corpse whose appearance is so wretched that none can look upon it without emotions of horror. Now, this is Satan's delight. He conceives death to be his masterpiece because of its terror and because of the ruin that it works. The greater the evil, the better he delights in it. No doubt he gloats over our sicknesses; he rejoices in our sin; but death is to him a theme of as much delight as he can be capable of in his eternal misery. He, as far as he can, shouts for joy when he witnesses how, by one piece of treachery, he has swept the world with the broom of destruction and hurried all men to the tomb.

Death is very lovely to the devil for another reason—not only because it is his chief work on earth but also because it gives him the finest opportunity in the world for the display of his malice and his craft. The devil is a coward, the greatest of cowards, as most wicked beings are. A Christian in health he will seldom attack; a Christian who has been living near his Master and is strong in grace the devil will leave alone, because he knows he will meet his match then; but if he can find a Christian either weak in faith or weak in body, he thinks it a fair opportunity for attack.

When death comes with all its terrors, it is usual for Satan to make a fierce inroad into the soul. Usually with many of the saints, if not in the last stage of death, yet some little time before it, there is a ferocious onslaught made by the great enemy of souls. And then he loves death, because death weakens the mind. The approach of death destroys some of the mental power and takes away from us for a season some of those spirits by which we have been cheered in better days. It makes us lie there, languid and faint and weary. Seeing his opportunity, the devil steals in upon us. Hence, I believe for this reason he is said to have the power of death, for I cannot believe that the devil has the power of death in any other sense but this, that it was originated by him and that he at such time generally displays the most of his malice and of his power. For it is certain that the devil has not the power of death so as to cause death. All the devils in hell could not take away the life of the smallest infant in the world, and though we lie gasping and sick so that the doctors despair of us, it is nothing but the design of the Almighty that can cause us to die, even in the extremity of our weakness. We rejoice to believe that an angel's arm cannot hurl us to the grave, even though it is the arm of that fallen archangel Lucifer. And we rejoice to know that afterward a myriad of angels cannot confine us there, so that neither for the locking of the door nor for the securing of it afterward does the devil have any power whatever over the Christian in death.

Many believers have such an understanding of faith that they conceive death to be a thing of happiness and pleasure and delight, and living near the fountain of all bliss, that is their God, their path is filled with sunshine, and their eye sparkles with perpetual happiness. They bear the trials of this life manfully as believers should; they take afflictions from the hand of God with all resignation and patience. Then the devil says, "It is of no use my meddling with that man with doubting thoughts; he is too mighty for me; he is powerful on his knees, and he is powerful with his God." "Hands off!" says the Christian to the devil then. But when we begin to be weak, when our mind through the influence of the body begins to be sad, when we misunderstand the purpose of God, then in our weakness the foe will beset us. For this reason, the devil looses death and has the power over it, because it is the time of nature's extremity, and therefore it is the time of the devil's opportunity.

Christ's Victory Over Satan's Power

The devil's power over death lies in three places, and we must look at it in three aspects. Sometimes the devil has power in death over the believer *by tempting him to doubt his resurrection* and leading him to look into the black future with the dread of annihilation. I will endeavor to show you that by the death of Christ that peculiar form of the devil's power in death is entirely removed. When the poor spirit lies on the verge of eternity, if faith is weak and the eyesight of hope is dim, the Christian will most likely look forward into what? Into a world unknown, and the language of even the unbeliever sometimes rushes into the lips of the most faithful child of God. You may tell him of the promises; you may try to cheer him by reminding him of certain revelations of the future. But apart from the death of Christ, even the Christian himself would look forward to death as being a dreary goal, a dark cloudy end to a life of weariness and woe.

Where am I speeding toward? The answer comes back: from blank nothingness you came, and you are speeding to the same; there is nothing for you; when you die you are forever lost. Or if reason has been well taught, it may perhaps reply to him, "Yes, there is another world, but reason can tell him only that it thinks so. It dreams of it, but what that other world shall be, what its tremendous mysteries, what its gorgeous splendor, or what its horrible terrors, reason cannot tell." The sting of death would be to such a man, who had no view of immortality of Christ, the thought that he was to be annihilated or, if to exist, that he knew not how or where.

The death of Christ has taken this all away. If I lie dying, Satan may come to me and say, "You are to be annihilated, you are now sinking beneath the waves of time, and you shall lie in the caverns of nothingness forever. Your living spirit is to cease to exist forever."

I would reply to him, "No, not so. I have no fear of your words, O Satan. Your power to tempt me here fails utterly and entirely. See there my Savior! He died—He died really and actually, for His heart was pierced; He was buried; He lay in His grave three days; but, O devil, He was not annihilated, for He rose again from the tomb on the third day, and in the glories of the resurrection He appeared unto many witnesses and gave infallible proofs that He was risen from the dead.

"And now, O Satan, I tell you that you cannot put an end to my existence, for you could not put an end to the existence of my Lord. As the Lord the Savior rose, so shall His followers. I say with Job, 'I know that my Redeemer liveth' (19:25), and therefore I know that though 'worms destroy this body, yet in my flesh shall I see God' (vs. 26). You tell me, O Satan, that I am to be swallowed up and be a thing of nothingness, but you are a liar. My Savior was not swallowed up, and yet He died; He died but could not long be held a prisoner in the tomb. Come, death, and bind me, but you cannot destroy me. Come, grave, open your ghastly mouth and swallow me up, but I shall burst your bonds another day. When that all-glorious morning shall dawn, I, having a dew like the dew of herbs upon me, shall be raised up and shall live in His sight. Because He lives I shall live also."

So, you see, Christ, by being a witness to the fact of the resurrection, has broken the power of the devil in death. In this respect He has prevented him from tempting us to fear annihilation, because as Christians, we believe that because Christ rose again from the dead, even so those who sleep in Jesus will the Lord bring with Him.

But now for a more common temptation—another phase of the devil's power in death. Often the devil comes to us in our lifetime and tempts us by *telling us that our guilt will certainly prevail against us*, that the sins of our youth and our former transgressions are still in our bones, and *that when we sleep in the grave our sins shall rise up against us*. "They have been many," says the devil, "and they have gone before you unto judgment, and others shall follow after." When the believer is weak and his heart and flesh fail him, were it not for the great doctrine of the death of Christ, the devil would be able to tempt him. Satan would say, "You are about to die. I dare not tell you that there is no future state, but while you have made a fine profession of Christ, I charge you that you have been a hypocrite.

You pretend that you are one of the Lord's beloved, but look at your sins. Remember that day when your rebellious lusts arose and you gave way to the transgression? How often did similar sins not occur?"

The devil takes up our diary, turns over the pages, and with an accusing finger points to our sins. Then he reads scornfully, with a leer upon his countenance. "See here saint," he hisses. "Saint! Ha! A fine saint you were." And he turns page after page, stopping over some very dark page to say, "See here!" He taunts the believer with the thing and says, "David, remember Bathsheba; Lot, remember Sodom and the cave; Noah, remember the vineyard and what the drunkenness did." It makes even the saint quiver when sin stares him in the face—when the ghosts of his old sins rise up and stare upon him. He is a man who has faith indeed who can look sin in the face and still say, "The blood of Jesus Christ cleanses me from sin."

Were it not for the blood, were it not for Jesus' death, you can easily imagine what power the devil would have over us in the hour of death, because he would fling all our sins in our teeth just when we came to die. But now through Christ's atonement, we reply to the temptation to sin, "In truth, O Satan, you are right. I have rebelled, I will not deny my conscience and my memory. I admit I have transgressed. Go ahead, turn the blackest page of my history, I confess all. But O fiend, go to Calvary's cross and see my substitute bleeding there. My sins were laid on His eternal shoulders, and He has cast them from His own shoulders into the depths of the sea. Be gone, hellhound! Would you worry me? Go and satisfy yourself with a sight of that Man who entered the gloomy dungeons of death and slept awhile there and then tore the bars away and led captivity captive as a proof that He was justified of God the Father and that I also am justified in Him." Yes, this is the way that Christ's death destroys the power of the devil.

"Ah!" said an aged saint once who had been much teased by Satan. "At last I got rid of my temptations, sir, and I enjoyed much peace." "How did you do it?" asked a Christian friend who visited him. "I showed him blood, sir; I showed him the blood of Christ." That is the thing the devil cannot endure. You may tell the devil, "Oh, but I have prayed so many times!" He will sniff at your prayers. You may tell him, "But I was a preacher." He will laugh in your face and tell you you preached your own damnation. You may tell him you had some good works, and he will lift them up and say, "These are your good works—filthy rags." He sneers at repentance and tears. But the moment you say, "Nothing in my hand I bring, simply to the cross I cling," it is all over with the devil then. There is nothing now that he can do, for the death of Christ has destroyed the power that the devil has over us to tempt us on account of guilt. "The sting of death is sin" (1 Cor. 15:56). Our Jesus took the sting away, and now death is harmless to us because it is not succeeded by damnation.

The evil one has another temptation for the believer. "It may be very true," the devil says, "that you are to live forever and that your sins have been pardoned. But you have often found it very hard to persevere, and now you are about to die and will be sure to fail. The little hornets you met in the past were enough to worry you, and now this death is the prince of dragons. It will be all over with you now. You know that when you used to go through a shallow stream of difficulty you were crying for fear of being drowned: what will you do now that you have got into the swelling of the Jordan? You were afraid of the lions when they were chained: what will you do with this unchained lion? In the fullness of strength and health you trembled at me: now I shall have at you, when I get you in your dying time and your strength fails. Once I get my grip on you, you will be overcome."

Sometimes the poor fainthearted believer thinks that it is true. But our sure answer should be, "O fiend, you tempted us to think that you will conquer us. Remember, Satan, that the strength that has preserved me against you has not been my own; the arm that has delivered me has not been my arm of flesh and blood, or I would have been overcome long ago. Look over there. See the omnipotent One. His Almightiness is the power that preserves to the end; and therefore, however weak I am, when I am weak, then I am strong, and in my last hour of peril I shall overcome you."

Notice again that this answer springs from Christ's death. Let us just picture the scene. When the Lord Jesus came down to earth, Satan knew His purpose. He knew that the Lord was the Son of God, and when he saw Him as an infant in the manger, he thought if he could kill Him and get Him in the bonds of death, what a fine thing it would be! So he stirred up the spirit of Herod to slay Him, but Herod missed his mark. Many times did Satan strive to put the personal existence of Christ in danger so that he might get Christ to die. Poor fool that he was, he did not know that when the divine died He would bruise the devil's head.

Once, you remember, when Christ was in the synagogue, the devil stirred up the people and made them angry; and he thought, "Oh, what a glorious thing it would be to kill Him, and then I would reign supreme forever." So he got the people to take Christ to the brow of the hill, and he gloated over the thought that now surely He would be cast down. But Christ escaped. Satan tried to starve Him in the desert temptation, and he tried to drown Him on the sea in a storm; but there was no starving or drowning Him, and Satan no doubt panted for His blood and longed that He would die.

At last the day arrived; it was telegraphed to the court of hell that at last Christ would die. They rang their bells with hellish mirth and joy. "He will die now," said he. "Judas has taken the thirty pieces of silver. Let those scribes and Pharisees get Him, and they will no more let Him go than the spider will a poor fly. We have Him now." The devil laughed with delight when he saw the Savior stand before Pilate's bar. When it was said, "Let him be crucified," the devil's joy knew no bounds except the bound that his own misery must ever set to it. In death, as Christ was seen of angels He was seen of devils, too; and that dreary march from Pilate's palace to the cross was one that devils saw with extraordinary interest. And when they saw Him on the cross, there stood the exulting fiend, smiling to himself. "Ah! I have the King of Glory now in my dominion; I have the power of death, and I have the power over the Lord Jesus." He exerted that power, till the Lord Jesus had to cry out in bitter anguish, "My God, my God, why hast thou forsaken me?"

How short-lived was the hellish victory! How brief was the satanic triumph! Jesus died, and "It is finished!" shook the gates of hell. Down from the cross the Conqueror leaped, pursued the fiend with thunderbolts of wrath; swift to the shades of hell the fiend did fly, and swift descending went the Conqueror after him. And seize him He did—chained him to His chariot wheel, dragged him up the steeps of glory, angels shouting all the while, "He hath led captivity captive, and gave gifts unto men" (Eph. 4:8).

Now, devil, you said you would overcome me when I come to die. Satan I defy and laugh you to scorn! My Master overcame you, and I shall overcome you yet. You say you will overcome the saint, do you? You could not overcome the saint's Master, and you will not overcome the saint. You thought you had conquered Jesus once: you were bitterly deceived. Now you think you shall overcome the little faith and the faint heart, but you are wondrously mistaken, for we shall assuredly tread Satan under our feet shortly. Even in our last extremity, with fearful odds against us, we shall be "more than conquerors through him that loved us."

You see, then, that Christ's death has taken away from Satan the advantage that he has over the saint in the hour of death, so that we may joyfully descend the shelving banks of the Jordan or may even, if God calls us to a sudden death, glide from its abrupt cliffs, for Christ is with us, and to die is gain.

Christ Has Thoroughly Taken Away Satan's Power

"That through death he might destroy him that had the power of death, that is, the devil." Death was the devil's primary entrenchment: Christ bearded the lion in his den and fought him in his own territory. When He took death from him and dismantled that once impregnable fortress, He took away from him not only that but also every other advantage that the devil had over the saint. And now Satan is a conquered foe, not only in the hour of death but also in every other hour and in every other place. He is an enemy, both cruel and mighty; but he is a foe who quakes and quails when a Christian gets into the ring with him, for he knows that though the fight may waver for a little while in the scale, the balance of victory must fall on the side of the saint, because Christ by His death destroyed the devil's power.

Satan may get much power over you by tempting you to indulge in the lusts of the flesh or in the pride of life; he may convince you to engage in dishonesty for financial gain; he may entice you to indulge in a pleasure; he may promise delights and satisfactions of tempting fruit that are accompanied with his old line that he will make you like a god. But the Christian says, "Satan, my Master died when He battled with you, and therefore I will have nothing to do with you. If you killed my Lord, you will kill me too if you can, and therefore away with you! But inasmuch as you lay down silver for me and tell me I can have it if I do wrong, lo, Satan, I can cover your silver with gold and have ten times as much to spare afterward. You say I shall reap a gain if I sin. No, but the treasures of Christ are greater riches than all the treasures of Egypt. If

146 / The Power of Christ the Warrior

you were to bring me a crown and say, 'There, you shall have that if you will sin,' I should say, 'What a poor crown! Why, Satan, I have got a better one than that laid up in heaven. I could not sin for such a paltry crown as you are offering.' " In he brings his bags of gold and says, "Now, sin and it's all yours." The believer says, "Why, that stuff is not worth my looking at. I have an inheritance in a city where the streets are paved with solid gold. Take your poor chinking bits and leave!" He brings in loveliness, and he tempts us by it, but we say to him, "Why, devil, what is loveliness to me? My eyes have seen the King in His beauty and the land that is very far off; and by faith I know that I shall go where beauty's self, even in her perfection, is excelled. My Savior is the chief among ten thousand and altogether lovely. That is no temptation for me! Christ has died, and I count all these things you show me but dross, that I may win Christ and be found in Him." So that you see, even in temptation, the death of Christ has destroyed the devil's power.

"You will not yield, will you?" says the devil. "You cannot be tempted! Well, if you cannot be drawn aside, I will pull you down. What are you, puny man, that you should stand against me? I have made angels fall, and I am not afraid of you. Come on!" And he puts his foot to our foot, and with his dragon yell he frights the echoes till they dare not reply. He lifts his blazing sword and thinks to smite us to the ground. You know, my brethren, what the shield is that must catch the blow. It is the shield of faith in Christ who died for us. Satan hurls his darts, but his darts hurt not, for we catch them also on this all-powerful shield, Christ and His cross, so that, let his insinuations be ever so direful, the death of Christ has destroyed the devil's power either to tempt or to destroy. Satan may be allowed to attempt either the one or the other, but he can be successful in neither. The death of Christ has destroyed him.

Some foolish people say they do not believe in a devil. I have only to tell them I don't believe in them, because if they knew themselves much they would very soon find a devil. But it is quite possible that they have very little evidence of there being any devil, for you know the devil never wastes his time. He comes down the street and sees a greedy, covetous man whose business it is to defraud widows and orphans. "Drive by," says the devil. "No need to stop there. The man needs no help. He will go to hell easily enough." Wherever he finds sin being engaged in, why should he trouble himself with the person?

But Satan finds a poor saint upon his knees, exercising but very little power in prayer. "Oh!" says he. "I will not have this creature at last, but I will howl at him now." There is a poor sinner just returning from his evil ways and crying, "I have sinned and done evil in God's sight; Lord, have mercy on me." "Losing a subject," says Satan. "I'll have him. I will not lose this one." So he worries the sinner.

The reason why a person doesn't believe there is a devil, very likely, is that the devil seldom comes to him because he is so safe that the devil does not take any trouble to look after him, and he has not seen the devil because he is too bad for him to care about. But when a man lives near to God, or when a man's conscience begins to be aroused, then Satan cries, "To arms!" for two good reasons: first, because he wants to worry him, and second, because he wants to destroy him. We may bless God that though the devil may direct his utmost scorn and craft and malice against the believer, the believer is safe behind the Rock Christ Jesus and may rest secure.

O children of God, death has lost its sting because the devil's power over it is destroyed. Then cease to fear dying. You know what death is: look him in the face and tell him you are not afraid of him. Ask God for grace that by an intimate knowledge and a firm belief in your Master's death, you may be strengthened for that dread hour. And mark me, if you so live, you may be able to think of death with pleasure and to welcome it when it comes with intense delight. It is sweet to die: to lie upon the bosom of Jesus and have one's soul kissed out of one's body by the lips of divine affection. And you who have lost friends or who may be bereaved, sorrow not as those who are without hope, for remember, the power of the devil is taken away. What a sweet thought the death of Christ brings us concerning those who are departed! They are gone, but do you know how far they have gone? The distance between glorified spirits in heaven and the saints on earth seems great, but it is not so. We are not far from home. One gentle sigh, and we are there on the eternal shore.

"All power is given unto me in heaven and in earth. Go ye therefore." I have met believers who have tried to read the Bible the wrong way. They have said, *"God has a purpose that is certain to be fulfilled, therefore we will not budge an inch. All power is in the hands of Christ, therefore we will sit still."* But that is not Christ's way of reading the passage. Based on His power, Christ tells us to go and do something. He puts us on the go because He has all power. I know that many of us have a tendency to say, *"Everything is wrong, the world gets darker and darker, and everything is going to the bad."* We sit and fret together in most delightful misery and try to cheer each other downward into greater depths of despair! Or, if we do stir ourselves a little, we feel that there is not much good in our service and that very little can possibly come of it. This message of our Master seems to me to be something like the sound of a trumpet. I have given you the strains of a harpsichord, but now there rings out the clarion note of a trumpet. Here is the power to enable you to *"go."* Therefore, *"go"* away from your melancholy and away from your ashes and your dust. Shake yourselves from your negative thoughts. The bugle calls, *"Up and away!"* The battle has begun, and every good soldier of Jesus Christ must be to the front for his Captain and Lord. Because all power is given to Christ, He passes on that power to His people and sends them forth to battle and to victory.

Chapter Twelve

Our Omnipotent Leader

And Jesus came and spake unto them, saying, All power is given unto me in heaven and in earth. Go ye therefore, and teach all nations, baptizing them in the name of the Father, and of the Son, and of the Holy Ghost: teaching them to observe all things whatsoever I have commanded you: and, lo, I am with you alway, even unto the end of the world—Matthew 28:18–20.

OUR SAVIOR WAS ALWAYS with His disciples until the time of His death. After His resurrection, He was with them often, but not always. He came and went mysteriously; the doors being shut, He was there suddenly when they least expected Him, or He appeared to them as they walked by the way or while they were fishing or when they came to the mountain in Galilee, the appointed rendezvous. On this particular occasion, the Savior made Himself very much at home with His disciples. According to a recent popular translation of the text, "Jesus came and talked unto them." He spoke to His disciples as a friend; He came into close contact with them in the friendliest familiarity. The glory of that time to them was that He was there and that He spoke with them. It does not matter where it was; He was there, and wherever He pleases to be the center of the group, there is sure to be a memorable gathering. This is how we should regard our gathering together as a church. The best meeting is when Christ is there and when He Himself by His divine Spirit speaks familiarly to our souls.

Notice what it was about that our Lord spoke to His disciples. He was going away from them; His bodily presence would no longer be enjoyed by His followers until He should so come in like manner as they were to see Him go up into heaven. But His last talk, or one of the last talks He ever had with them before His ascension, was about Himself and His work. It was a time of taking them into His confidence, explaining to them the partnership that the Father had established between Him and them and making them to know the fellowship with the Father and with His Son Jesus Christ that was now to cover the whole of their lives. You see, He begins by speaking to them about His own power: "All power is given unto me in heaven and in earth." We are not prepared to go out to work for Christ until we truly know Him ourselves and also know something of the divine power that He is prepared to give to us. It is well for us to learn the lesson ourselves before we attempt to teach it to others. Do not go into the nations until you have first gone into your closet and had fellowship with the Master Himself; you will blunder in your errand unless you go forth fresh from His blessed presence.

What were they to do but to act for Him? "Go ye therefore, and teach all nations." They were to teach those nations only about Him; He was to be the great subject of all their teaching. The correct word is *disciple* all nations. They were to disciple them, to make them not their own disciples but His disciples; He was to still be the Teacher, the Rabbi, the Master; they were only to go forth to do His work, not their own. Beware of forming a party of which you shall be the head; abhor the very thought of any such action. We must gather the nations to Him; otherwise, we are not His servants, we are our own masters. We are renegades and disloyal if we do that.

They were to baptize those who were made disciples, but it was to be in His name in association with that of the Father and of the Holy Spirit. He who is not baptized into the name of the Lord Jesus Christ is not baptized at all; the name of Christ is inseparably linked with those who are baptized according to the scriptural fashion. So, you see, whether it is preaching or discipling or baptizing, we must keep close to Christ. It is all along that line; we preach Him, we make disciples for Him, we baptize in His name.

When those who were made disciples were baptized, what was next to be done? "Teaching them to observe all things whatsoever I have commanded you." The shepherding of the sheep must still be in our Lord's name. We do not plant a church in any other name but His, neither do we know any rule or order or book of discipline but that which He has left us. He alone is King in Zion, and only what He teaches is authoritative. The explanations given by His servants we must judge by the tests He has given to us, but the Word of the Master is to be obeyed and accepted in its entirety. There is no true work done for Christ unless we always put Him in His right place as the omnipotent Leader and Commander of His people and ourselves as His servants in all things, seeking even in the smallest matters to be obedient to His revealed will.

Do not fail to notice that all this is to be done in association with Himself: "Lo, I am with you alway." "Do all that I have commanded you, but you must also ever have Me at your side. You will do nothing worth the doing, you will spend your life in failure, unless you keep up perpetual communion with Me. Lo, I am with you always." This must be the case until this dispensation closes, and it shall close only by our being with Christ in a still higher sense. We shall then go from His being with us to our being with Him, from spiritual fellowship to an actual, visible, corporeal fellowship. We shall be like Him when we shall see Him as He is (1 John 3:2). He shall stand in the latter day upon the earth (Job 19:25), He shall reign among His ancients gloriously (Isa. 24:23); and until then, it is our privilege to abide at His side and to never venture forth except we feel that He goes with us, making our discipling in His name to be of effect upon the hearts and consciences of men.

I will have missed my purpose in this preface if I have not said that if any of us would receive a commission for Christian service, it must come from Christ Himself; if we would carry out that commission, it must be in loyalty to Christ; and if we hope to succeed in that commission, it must be in a perpetual, personal fellowship with Christ. We must begin to work with Him and go on working with Him and never cease to work until He Himself shall come to discharge us from the service because there is no further need of it. Oh, that we did all our church work in the name of the great Head of the Church! Oh, that we did all Christ's work consciously in the presence and in the strength of Christ!

Still only introducing my main theme, I ask you to consider the Savior's grand statement: "All power is given unto me in heaven and in earth." *All power*. Read it, if you like, *all authority*. It is not so much force that is meant, as moral power. Christ at this moment possesses a royal authority—by might, it is true, but chiefly by right. His is the power that comes of His merits, of His glorious nature, and of the gift of the divine Spirit who rests upon Him without measure. The word we translate *power* has a wider meaning than that; you find a good example of it in John 1:12: "But as many as received him, to them gave he power to become the sons of God," where the word *power* might be rendered *privilege* or *right* or *liberty* and yet is correctly translated *power* also. Christ at this moment has all rights in heaven and in earth; He has all sovereignty and dominion, and, of course, He has all the might that backs up His right. But it is not mere power in the sense of force; it is not the dynamite power in which earthly kings delight; it is another and a higher kind of force that Christ has, even the divine energy of love. He possesses at this moment all authority in heaven and in earth.

"All power," He says, "is given unto me." You and I are not sent out to preach the gospel to get power for Christ; He has it now. We are not sent out, as we sometimes say, to win the world for Christ; in the strictest sense, it is His now. He is the King of glory at this very moment; He is even now Lord over all, King of kings and Lord of lords with all authority. Our Lord Jesus holds in His hand the scepter that gives Him power over all flesh that He may give eternal life to as many as the Father has given Him. He has already in His hand that scepter with which He shall break the nations as with a rod of iron and dash them in pieces as a potter's vessel. He does not need to go up to His throne; He is already enthroned. He does not need to be crowned; He is already crowned.

All power is not merely the power Christ possesses naturally by His Godhead or a power that could be compassed entirely by His manhood, for that must necessarily be limited; but it is a power that can be contained within that blessed complex Person, the Christ of God. It is as the God-man, the Mediator between God and men, that all might is bestowed upon Him as the reward of the travail of His soul, so that now He can say that boundless authority has been given to Him.

All power in heaven belongs to Christ, that is, all power with God. You remember how Elijah prayed and opened heaven by his prayers, but the Christ of God is greater than Elijah. You know how men of God have been blessed with remarkable force and energy in their pleadings, but the intercessions of Christ are more powerful than all the intercessions of His people. Actually, they are the power that gives effect to all the intercessions of all the saints. It is He who puts power into them and into their petitions. Of course, as Christ has power with God, so has He power over all the holy angels and all pure intelligences. All power of every kind that has to do with heavenly things and heavenly places is in the hand of Christ.

Christ has all power also in earth. That is to say, He is Lord over all the earth. "The sea is his, and he made it: and his hands formed the dry land" (Ps. 95:5). He is Master of all providences; His hand ever holds the helm and steers the ship that carries His disciples. He is Master of all kings and of all politics, and when at times we tremble for our beloved nation, there is no real need for us to do so. "The LORD reigneth; let the earth rejoice; let the multitude of isles be glad thereof" (Ps. 97:1). Christ has all authority over all the sons of men and all the forces of nature. From the stars that light up the brow of midnight to the deepest law that works in the bowels of the earth, the Lord Jesus Christ is Master of them all. All power, He says, is given to Him in heaven and in earth.

We Greatly Rejoice in Christ

I do not know that our divine Master could have said anything to us that would have made our hearts thrill with a sweeter delight than we derive from these words: "All power is given unto me." Beloved, do you not wish all power to be given to *Him whom we love*? I confess that nothing makes me rejoice more than the fact that He reigns. I do not feel any sorrow so much as the sorrow of seeing His truth trodden into the mire, and I know no joy that ever thrills my soul like that of knowing that still is Jesus set as King upon the holy hill of Zion, that still He reigns, and that "he must reign, till he hath put all enemies under his feet" (1 Cor. 15:25). Is there any power you would like to keep back from Him? Is it not the delight of our soul to think that even while He dwelt here among men Jesus could say to His poor disciples, "All power is given unto me." Do we not feel ready to shout, "Hallelujah! Hallelujah!" when we know that this is really a fact?

We delight to know that all power is in the hands of Christ, because we are sure that *it will be used correctly*. Power in the hands of some people is dangerous, but power in the hands of Jesus is blessed. Let Him have all power! Let Him do what He will with it, for He cannot will anything but that which is right and just and true and good. Give Him unbounded sovereignty. We want no limited monarchy when Christ is King; no, put every crown on that dear head, and let Him have unrestricted sway, for there is none like Him. He is more glorious than all the sons of men, and it is our joy to know that all power is given unto Him.

This also furnishes us with *good reasons for often going to Him.* I love to think that all power is in Him, and none in me, for now I cannot keep away from Him. I am obliged to knock at His door, and if He asks me why I come so often, I must answer, "It cannot be helped, my Lord, for all power is with You. If I had power to provide for myself, I might try to do so, but since without You I should die of hunger, I must come to You for every breath and every pulse." Yes, it is even so; because all power is given to Christ, we rejoice that we may always go to Him. Will you criticize a baby because it longs for its mother's milk? How can it live without its natural nourishment? And can you criticize our feebleness because it loves to hang upon the omnipotence of Christ?

We are glad that all power is given to Him because *He is so easy to access.* It is difficult for those in need to speak with kings, but it is not difficult for them to tell their needs to the King of kings. His door is always open to petitioners, and His ear and heart are ever ready to listen to their needs. Call upon Him whenever you will— He will not send you away. Come to His strength whenever you may, that strength will flow out to your weakness and make you strong in the Lord and in the strength of His might.

We See the Practical Outcome of This Truth

"All power is given unto me in heaven and in earth. Go ye therefore." I have met believers who have tried to read the Bible the wrong way. They have said, "God has a purpose that is certain to be fulfilled, therefore we will not budge an inch. All power is in the hands of Christ, therefore we will sit still." But that is not Christ's way of reading the passage. Based on His power, Christ tells us to go and do something. He puts us on the go because He has all power. I know that many of us have a tendency to say, "Everything is wrong, the world gets darker and darker, and everything is going to the bad." We sit and fret together in most delightful misery and try to cheer each other downward into greater depths of despair! Or, if we do stir ourselves a little, we feel that there is not much good in our service and that very little can possibly come of it. This message of our Master seems to me to be something like the sound of a trumpet. I have given you the strains of a harpsichord, but now there rings out the clarion note of a trumpet. Here is the power to enable you to "go." Therefore, "go" away from your melancholy and away from your ashes and your dust. Shake yourselves from your negative thoughts. The bugle calls, "Up and away!" The battle has begun, and every good soldier of Jesus Christ must be to the front for his Captain and Lord. Because all power is given to Christ, He passes on that power to His people and sends them forth to battle and to victory.

Yet there is another note in this trumpet call: "Go *ye*." Who is to go out of that first band of disciples? It is Peter, the rash and headstrong. It is John, who sometimes wishes to call fire from heaven to destroy men. It is Philip, with whom the Savior has been so long and yet he has not known Him. It is Thomas, who must put his finger into the print of the nails or he will not believe. Yet the Master says to them, "Go ye; all power is given unto Me; therefore go. You are as good for My purpose as anybody else would be. There is no power in you, I know, but then all power is in Me; therefore go." "Fear not, thou worm Jacob, and ye men of Israel; I will help thee, saith the LORD, and thy redeemer, the Holy One of Israel. Behold, I will make thee a new sharp threshing instrument having teeth: thou shalt thresh the mountains, and beat them small, and shalt make the hills as chaff" (Isa. 41:14–15).

"But, Lord, if we go to men, *they will ask for our passports.*" "Take them," says Christ, "for all authority is given to Me. You are free of heaven, and you are free of earth. There is no place—whether it is far-off Ethiopia or the deserts of Scythia or in the center of Rome—where you may not go. My authority is all the passport that you need."

"But, Lord, *we need a commission.*" "There is your commission," says the Lord. "All power is given unto Me, and I delegate it to you. I have authority, and I give you authority; go therefore because I have the authority. Go and teach princes and kings and beggars, teach them all alike. I ordain you, I authorize you, as many of you as know Me and have My love shed abroad in your hearts. I commission you to go and tell others of the dear Savior you have found, and if they ask how you dare to do it, tell them not that the bishop ordained you or a synod licensed you but that all power is given to your Master in heaven and in earth, and you have come in His name."

"Moreover," says the Master, "*I send you with My power gone before you.*" Christ does not say, "Go and win the power for Me on earth, go and get power for Me among the sons of men." No, but He says, "All authority and power are already vested in Me; go ye therefore. I send you to a country that is not an alien kingdom; I send you to a country that is Mine, for all souls are Mine. If you go to the Jews or to the Gentiles, they are Mine; if it is to India or China that you go, you need ask no man's approval; you are in your own King's country, you are on your own King's errand, you have your own King's power going before you." I do believe that often, when missionaries go to a country, they have rather to gather ripe fruit than to plant trees. As the Lord sent the hornets to clear the way for the children of Israel, so does He often send singular changes—political, social, and religious—before the heralds of the cross to prepare the way for them; and this is the message that sounds with clear clarion note to all the soldiers of King Jesus; "I have all authority; therefore, without misgivings or questionings, go and evangelize all nations, baptizing them in the name of the Father, and of the Son, and of the Holy Spirit."

We Feel the Need of It

If anyone knows the power that is in Christ to make his ministry of any use, I am sure that I do! I hardly ever come to the pulpit without bemoaning myself that I ever should have been called to a task for which I seem more unfit than any other man who was ever born. Woe is me that I should have to preach a gospel that so overmasters me and that I feel that I am so unworthy to preach! Yet I could not give it up, for it were a far greater woe to me not to preach the gospel of Jesus Christ.

Unless the Holy Spirit blesses the Word, we who preach the gospel are of all men most miserable, for we have attempted a task that is impossible; we have entered upon a sphere where nothing but the supernatural will ever avail. If the Holy Spirit does not renew the hearts of our hearers, we cannot do it. If He does not send the truth home into the soul, we might as well speak into the ear of a corpse. All that we have to do is quite beyond our unaided power; we must have our Master with us, or we can do nothing. We deeply feel our need of this great truth. We do not merely say it, but we are driven every day by our own deep sense of need to rejoice that our Lord has declared that He has the power we need. Every kind of power that there is in heaven and in earth we shall need before we can fully discharge this ministry. Before the nations shall be brought to hear the gospel of Christ, before the testimony of Him shall be borne in every land, we shall need the whole omnipotence of God; we shall want every force in heaven and earth before this is done. Thank God that this power is all laid by ready for our use, the strength that is equal to such a stupendous task as this is already provided.

We Believe and Rest in This Word

We believe in this power of Christ, and we rest in it. *We do not seek any other power.* There is a craving, often, after great intellectual power; people want "clever" men to preach the gospel. I fear that the gospel has suffered more damage from clever men than from anything else. I question whether the devil himself has ever worked so much mischief in the Church of God as clever men have done. We want to have such mental vigor as God pleases to give us, but we remember the Word, "Not by might, nor by power, but by my spirit, saith the Lord of hosts" (Zech. 4:6). The world is not going to be saved by worldly wisdom or by fine oratory; brilliant speeches and poetic periods do not win souls for Christ. The power to do this is the power that is in Christ; and the Church of God, when she is in her right senses, does not look for any other power. She does not look to kings and presidents to sanction her message. The Church of God has a kingdom that is not of this world. All power for the extension of the kingdom of Christ is in Himself. His own person sustains His own kingdom, and we will not go to any other fountain of authority to draw the power we need. The Church of Christ must always say to Him, "All my springs are in thee" (Ps. 87:7).

We believe and rest in this truth, *defying every other power.* Every other power that can be imagined may set itself against the kingdom of Christ; but it does not matter, no, not one whistle of the wind, for all power is already in Christ, and that which seems to oppose His kingdom must be but the mere empty name of power. There can be no real power about it, for all power is in Him both in heaven and in earth.

This being so, we rest quite sure that *even our weaknesses will not hinder the progress of His kingdom.* Rather, we glory in our weaknesses, for now the power of Christ will become more con-spicuous. The less we have by which the kingdom might be thought to be extended, the more clearly it will be seen that the kingdom is extended by the power of the King Himself.

At the same time, *all power that we have we give to Him*, because all power is His; and all power that we ever possess, we lay it under tribute to Him. What there is of good or of brightness or of light or of talent or of knowledge of this world, we say, "It all belongs to Jesus," and we set the broad arrow of our great King upon it and claim it as His.

O dear friend, why are we ever cast down? Why do we ever begin to question the ultimate success of the good cause? Why do we ever go home with aching head and palpitating heart because of the evils of the day? Courage, my brethren, courage; the King has all power; it is impossible to defeat Him. A great soldier just fell now, I know, and across the battlefield I see the clouds of smoke. The right wing of our army may be shattered for a moment, but the King in the center of the host still rides upon the white horse of vic-tory, and He has but to will it, He has but to speak a single word, and the enemy shall be driven away like chaff before the wind.

We Obey Him

Christ says, "Go." Then, *let us go at once*, according to His Word, in the track that God's own hand marks out for us. Let us go and disciple all nations; let us tell them that they are to learn of Christ and that they are to be obedient in His will. Let us also bap-tize those who become His disciples, as He bids us do: "baptizing them in the name of the Father, and of the Son, and of the Holy Ghost."

Next, *let us be loyal to Him in all things*, and let us train up His disciples in loyalty to Him: "teaching them to observe all things whatsoever I have commanded you." As He has all authority, let us not intrude another authority. Let us keep within the Master's house and seek to know the Master's mind, to learn the Master's will, to study the Master's Book, and to receive the Master's Spirit, and let these be dominant over all other power. And all the while *let us endeavor to keep in fellowship with Him*: "lo, I am with you alway." Let us never go away from Him. Let us be the servants who unloose the latches of His shoes, who bring water to His feet, and who count ourselves highly honored to be so close to Him.

Let us always keep *expecting Him to return.* The last words of the chapter suggest this thought: "Even unto the end of the world" or "of the age." You know that this age is to end with a glorious beginning of a brighter and better age; therefore, let us keep looking for it. Servants, you will not serve well unless you expect your Master's return. Let that expectation keep your lamps trimmed and your lights burning, for perhaps this very moment there will be heard in our streets the cry: "Behold, the bridegroom cometh; go ye out to meet him" (Matt. 25:6). May we all be so ready that this cry would be the sweetest music that our ears could ever hear!